STUDIES IN LITERATURE

I
EVANGELICAL RELIGION AND LITERATURE

Dominus noster Christus veritatem se non consuetudinem cognominavit.

Tertullian, *De virg. vel.* i.

I

EVANGELICAL RELIGION AND LITERATURE

Why has evangelical religion fared so badly in English literature? There can hardly be any question that it has fared badly, and it may be both interesting and instructive to speculate on the reasons why.

The fact is there, and everyone who is reasonably familiar with our literature must have observed it. The readiest example of it, and the largest, is the way that the great religious movements of the seventeenth and eighteenth centuries have been treated in fiction. For fiction, of all the forms of literature, presents the broadest judgement of life; in the phrase of a brilliant Frenchman, it is 'the metaphor of a philosophy.' It will be found that, in classical English fiction, the representatives of evangelical religion have been misrepresented and maligned in almost every instance.

Think, for example, of the prejudiced fashion in which Scott has dealt with Roundheads and Cavaliers, with Covenanters and their persecutors, with the Presbyterian ministry and the clergy of other Churches. Scott's Puritans and Covenanters and Cameronians are unlovely zealots at the best, and at the worst they are murderous fanatics. Probably his most favourable character of the sort is David Deans, in *The Heart of Midlothian*, and he is a very harsh type, strictly upright, but stern, obstinate, and censorious.

9

Most of the other portraits are much worse, as the mere mention of General Harrison, Major Bridgenorth, and Balfour of Burley is enough to show—men whose religion ranged between adamantine bigotry and sheer mania. A Presbyterian minister in the novels is usually a pedant or a fanatic. We can scarcely recall a favourable example, except Dr. Erskine at the Greyfriars in Edinburgh, when Colonel Mannering went there with Pleydell the lawyer, and the unnamed preacher heard by Frank Osbaldistone in the crypt of Glasgow Cathedral. On the other hand, Scott depicts sympathetically enough the Catholic priests and the Anglican clergy who figure in his pages.

This aspect of his work almost presents us with a psychological problem. Sir Walter Scott was one of the most chivalrous men that ever breathed ; he was incapable of deliberate vilification. But in this matter the literary tradition and his own social dislikes seem to have overcome both his discernment of character and his sense of justice. For there cannot be a moment's doubt that in all this region his work is so strongly prejudiced as to be false. No one would ever suspect from Scott's sketches of Puritans that Milton was a Puritan,[1] or from his treatment of the Covenanters that they numbered amongst them some of the best and bravest Scots of the age, or from his caricatures of preachers that the Presbyterian clergy of Scotland have always been, as they are to-day, the most able and the most learned ministry in Christendom.

On the whole, Methodism is treated with a similar

---

[1] Notwithstanding the passage in *Woodstock* in which Colonel Everard quotes *Comus* to Sir Henry Lee.

contempt in the eighteenth-century novelists, though the treatment is slighter, and a little respect seems to lurk occasionally amid the scorn. This last is curiously true alike of Richardson, of Fielding, and of Smollett. Richardson does not introduce any Methodists as characters in his novels, and has only a few allusions to Methodism, mostly slight and ironical. One of these, however, in *Sir Charles Grandison*, is distinctly complimentary, for Lady Charlotte writes: ' I am sorry that our own clergy are not as zealously in earnest as the Methodists. They have really, my dear, if we may believe Aunt Eleanor, given a face of religion to subterranean colliers, tinners, and the most profligate of men, who hardly ever before heard either of the word or thing. But *I* am not turning *Methodist*, Harriet ! No, you will not suspect me.'

Fielding depicts the imprisoned Methodist in *Amelia* as a canting hypocrite, and when describing the Bell Inn at Gloucester, in *Tom Jones*, he goes out of his way to tell us that the host is ' brother to the great preacher Whitefield, but is absolutely untainted with the pernicious principles of Methodism, or of any other heretical sect.' Blifil, a contemptible character in the same novel, is said to have ' lately turned Methodist, in hopes of marrying a very rich widow of the sect.' On the other hand, the mistress of the house where Jones went after the masquerade is said, later on, to have become a Methodist, whereupon, after ' rebuking Lady Bellaston very severely for her past life,' she had refused to have anything more to do with that detestable person's amours.

Smollett deals with Methodism in rather more detail.

Humphry Clinker, the hero of his last novel, is supposed to be a Methodist. Though his religion is ridiculed, he is described as a faithful servant, and a brave and worthy man. When he is falsely accused of having robbed a coach, and is sent to prison at Clerkenwell, the gaoler complains, with a perfect tempest of oaths, of the change in the prison since he came—there has been nothing but canting and praying, not a cask of beer nor a dozen of wine has been sold, and ' two or three as bold hearts as ever took the air upon Hounslow have been blubbering all night ! ' His master declares that ' if there were anything like affectation or hypocrisy in this excess of religion I would not keep Clinker in my service, but the fellow's character is downright simplicity, warmed with a kind of enthusiasm.' In the same novel the unpleasant spinster, Tabitha Bramble, and her illiterate waiting-woman, Winifred Jenkins, are also described as Methodists.

It is not surprising, when we remember the temper of the age, that unsympathetic caricatures of Methodists are found in these contemporary novelists. They are nothing like as scurrilous as the attacks upon Methodism that were made on the boards of the theatre, and in the pages of Calvinist theologians. While far enough from being fair, Fielding and Smollett are not so misleading and mischievous in their treatment of Methodists, upon the whole, as Scott in his representation of the Covenanters, or even as Thackeray in his portraiture of the later Evangelicals.

For the traditional prejudice manifests itself also in Thackeray, wherever he touches upon evangelical

religion. An outstanding example is his treatment of
the household of Mrs. Newcome, the Colonel's step-
mother, at Clapham. Thackeray's mind was essentially
tolerant, and it is plain that he makes an effort to do
justice to that lady's stern sense of duty and her
lavish charities. But the Hermitage is anything but
an attractive interior, filled as it is with ' preachers
daily bawling for hours,' with ' florid rhapsodists be-
labouring cushions with wearisome benedictions,' with
richly-laden tables ' surrounded by stout men in black,
with baggy white neck-cloths, who took the little boy
between their knees, and questioned him as to his
right understanding of the place whither naughty boys
were bound.'

It is much the same in *Vanity Fair*, with the account
of Lady Southdown, whose belief ' accommodated
itself to a prodigious variety of opinion, taken from
all sorts of doctors among the dissenters,' a few samples
of whom are engagingly catalogued as ' the Reverend
Saunders M'Nitre, the Scotch divine, the Reverend
Luke Waters, the mild Wesleyan, and the Reverend
Giles Jowls, the illuminated cobbler, who dubbed
himself Reverend as Napoleon crowned himself Emperor.' There is another name that it would be
a pity to omit from this outrageous list, for we are
told that Lady Emily ' was secretly attached to the
Reverend Silas Hornblower, who was tattooed in the
South Sea Islands ' !

Here, again, there can be no doubt at all as to the
essential falsity of these caricatures. The Clapham
evangelicals may not have made religion as attractive
as they ought, but Thackeray's rather venomous

sketches do no sort of justice to the historic fact that men like Henry Thornton, William Wilberforce, and Zachary Macaulay were the actual types of the people in question.

Indeed, evangelical religion has almost always been identified, as these names suggest, with the cause of liberty and humanity, and with the general current of progress in the world. Yet it has always received scant mercy from men of letters. While, on the other hand, the Catholic type of religion, though it has stood sponsor to many lost causes, which have been marked by much cruelty and wrong, has often been idealized in our fiction and our poetry.

Why is this? One reason has already been hinted. In some instances, the very fact that the cause was a lost cause has helped to glorify it. Little pity would have been wasted on Mary Queen of Scots, if she had grown old at Holyrood, and John Knox might have been a more popular figure with the novelists if he had been hanged in the Grassmarket. If Charles I had died in his bed, a detested tyrant, and Oliver Cromwell had been beheaded on Tower Hill, a martyred patriot, the glamour attached to the cause of the Cavaliers and the Jacobites would never have existed, and the Roundheads might have had a share of romance instead, which would certainly have reacted upon the literary treatment of Puritan religion. But this does not carry us far. It does not apply at every point, and other reasons must be sought.

One of these is undeniably the fact that evangelical religion has always made for strictness of behaviour. The world, in the apostolic sense of the word, that is to say, the gross mass of mankind, has always loved drink, dancing, the drama, races, games of chance ; religion of the evangelical type has always more or less frowned upon these things, and, as we think, with much justification.   But nobody is hated like a spoil-sport, and even abstention implies rebuke.   The world piped to our evangelical fathers, and those stern men would not respond.   Naturally the world resented their aloofness, and the worldling said, with a gibe, ' Dost thou think, because thou art virtuous, there shall be no more cakes and ale ? '

Literature, which largely reflects the spirit of the world, has reflected the worldly man's dislike of the strictness of evangelical piety.   A party of careless Cavaliers, laughing, drinking, playing dice, and making love, is a more congenial subject for literature than a Puritan conventicle full of grave men with Bibles in their hands.   Vice can be made piquant a good deal more easily than virtue.   It is a much lighter task to write an interesting history of plots and revolutions and wars than one of peace and prosperity.   ' The low sun makes the colour.'   There is no doubt that in one way ' the roses and raptures of vice ' lend them-selves more easily to literature, because they commend themselves more readily to the natural man, than the pure beauty and the unworldly happiness of earnest religion.

Then evangelical religion, in the earlier days, always spoke its own dialect.   It had an accent and a vocabulary of its own, largely derived from Scripture. The language of Canaan was one speech, and the Attic of literature was another.   This has counted for much.

John Foster realized it, and in his famous essay, *On the Aversion of Men of Taste to Evangelical Religion,* he pleaded for the abandonment of the patois of piety. He was unfortunate, however, in some of his particular suggestions. As an example of this, he would have substituted 'virtue' for 'righteousness'—a mere concession to the fashion of his day, and a very unhappy exchange, as Coleridge rightly felt. Nevertheless there was much reason in the general plea. For there is a religious jargon, in every age, which is merely ugly, and does nothing but harm. Naturally it offends every instinct of the man of letters, for whom words are living things, with delicate colours and graceful contours, with subtle and haunting values. That every religious writer should possess John Bunyan's or Jeremy Taylor's gift of style (to select widely separate exemplars) is past praying for. But every man who writes on religion ought at least to be able to address the cultivated people of his generation without offending their literary sense. This does not mean the mere secularization of style. There is much to be said on the other side of that question. It is significant that the writers of the New Testament seem deliberately to have avoided, as far as they could, the classical words for virtue, ἀρετή, manners, ἤθη, love, ἔρως, and happiness, εὐδαιμονία. Within limits, the religion of Christ discarded the words that had been demoralized by worldly use, and selected its own speech to express its own experience. And still, when religion adventures itself in the fields of literature, it must exercise some choice both of style and of vocabulary. It must, to some extent, speak its own idiom in every age.

Then it happens that religion of the evangelical type is less picturesque, on a superficial view, than the Catholic type of Christianity.   An ancient abbey and a gorgeous ritual, with splendid colour and solemn music, make a more sensuous appeal than a bare conventicle and an austere devotion.   It is true that the finer mind will often be able to discern spiritual beauty and spiritual reality beneath the plain exterior of evangelical religion, and will sometimes suspect a subtle spirit of worldliness masquerading in the guise of dignified worship.   But it is only the finer spirit that can do this.   For those who cannot see beneath the surface the contrast will remain.   As Leslie Stephen has well said : ' Shallow-minded people fancy Puritans to be prosaic because the laces and ruffles of the Cavaliers are a more picturesque costume at a masked ball than the dress of the Roundheads.   The Puritan has become a grim and ugly scarecrow on whom every buffoon may break his jest.   But the genuine old Puritan spirit ceases to be picturesque only because of its sublimity ; its poetry is sublimed into religion.'

It should be pointed out, however, that even this superficial element of the picturesque is to some extent a matter of prejudiced selection.   Evangelical religion is not always so ugly in its external circumstances, nor Catholic religion always so picturesque, as it has been the tradition of English letters to allege.

There is a characteristic example of this in Matthew Arnold's essay on Eugénie de Guérin.   He draws a malicious contrast between the setting of her life and that of Emma Tatham, who was regarded by some people, sixty years ago, as a poetess.   He deftly

2

suggests a picture of the Catholic girl of Languedoc, listening to the *nadalet* at Noël, and reading the legends of the saints. Then he describes the Methodist girl attending ' Hawley Square Chapel at Margate,' with its accompaniments—' the young female teachers of the Sunday School,' ' a venerable class-leader,' and so on. Now does not everyone see, after a moment's reflection, that this artful dig at the presumed ugliness of religious life among Protestants and Methodists is merely an example of what the psychologists call ' selective attention ' ? The writer has picked out a few circumstances in the one life which look picturesque and graceful largely because they are foreign, and a few circumstances in the other life which look banal, because they are English and familiar. The whole effect of contempt is in the selection. It would be quite possible, and perhaps amusing, to play that game the other way round. Let the Catholic girl go through the back streets of Leeds to a dingy Catholic chapel adorned with hideous oleographs of the Sacred Heart, and let the Methodist girl walk in the moonlight through a haunted glen to a Methodist chapel on the snowy fells, for the Watch Night, in the last hours of the year. The illusion of romance and banality in piquant contrast has simply been reversed. But it is as fair one way as the other.

Then the straiter sect of evangelicals, in past generations, were hostile to almost all literature that was not expressly religious. The drama was absolutely vetoed, and with the Restoration theatre in mind we cannot wonder. Fiction was also forbidden, with a rare exception like *The Fool of Quality*, because John

Wesley had approved it, and *Coelebs in Search of a Wife*, because it had been written by the blameless Hannah More. Poetry was in a little better case. Milton, Cowper, and Young were allowed, because the subjects of their poems were biblical, or because the tone of most of their verse was religious. And there, or thereabouts, ran the boundary. Everything else was suspect ; it was regarded as less than edifying, to say the least. Now this ban on literature had its inevitable reaction in more ways than one. Letters, despised by religion, learned to despise religion. The evangelical faith and the evangelical piety failed to secure any representation in literature other than a hostile and contemptuous one. Even that was not the whole extent of the penalty. For those who exiled themselves from the realm of letters became incapable of expressing themselves in a literary fashion. *Sic Amyclas, cum tacerent, perdidit silentium.* There is a brilliant exception in the case of the Wesleys and of some of the early Methodist preachers, but otherwise the voluminous literature of the Evangelical Revival is ' a continent of mud,' to borrow a phrase of Robert Hall's. Despite its real piety and its occasional learning it is one dead level of platitude. It is without any charm of imagination or any grace of style, and it is simply unread and unreadable to-day. All this is nothing less than a calamity. It is the result of a mistaken and unnecessary sacrifice of the graces of the mind. That error belongs to the past, and is not likely to be repeated.

But it is only fair to remember that religion, if it is earnest, and therefore evangelical religion especially, does necessarily impose some restraint and renunciation upon literature. It bans what St. Augustine called ' undisciplined words,' *verba indisciplinata.* When Dr. Johnson was talking of Foote, he said, ' He has wit. Then he has a great range for wit ; he never lets truth stand between him and a jest, and he is sometimes mighty coarse. Garrick is under many restraints from which Foote is free.' What was true of that disreputable buffoon is true in a much wider range. The very reverence and purity which religion presupposes are a restraint not only upon cynical wit and careless humour, but upon the spirit of reckless paradox and the brilliance that cares for nothing but itself. Religion forbids both to the imagination and the pen many a piquant situation and many a perilous experiment. As Tertullian said, ' What we are forbidden to do, the soul pictures to itself at its peril.' The ' arrogant intellectuality ' of which Nietzsche wrote (and which found expression in a writer like Oscar Wilde) is manifestly impossible to a humble disciple of Christ.

Then another large factor, undoubtedly, has been the snobbishness which attaches to the English character. Dissent has been the mainstay of evangelical religion in this country in a way that does not apply to any other of the Protestant nations. And Dissent was a revolt against established authority ; it was cruelly penalized for centuries, it was excluded from the universities, it worshipped in homely buildings, and it found its main support in the middle classes. For all these reasons it was disliked and despised by the governing caste, by the clergy, by the world of art and learning and letters ; and a legend of contempt was created that grew with the years and survives until the present day. It is probable that nobody ever existed in the least like Mr. Stiggins or Mr. Chadband, but Dickens was only prolonging (and exaggerating in his characteristic way), a convention which dated from the Restoration drama, and descended through the fiction of the eighteenth century, according to which every dissenter was an unctuous hypocrite.

This perverse legend has had some weird results in our history and our literature. Macaulay complained that he had read histories of England, dealing with the reign of George II, in which the rise of Methodism was never even mentioned, and expressed the hope that in a generation or two that breed of authors would be extinct. The birth of the Evangelical Revival was incomparably the most important thing that happened in that reign, and yet these historians thought it beneath their notice. It was a species of fanaticism among the lower orders that could expect no mention in a serious author.   It was not respectable. The young officer who was to become the victor of Waterloo changed his name from Wesley to Wellesley, for it would never have done for a subaltern in 1790 to be thought related to the founder of Methodism. When Cowper wanted to refer to Whitefield he veiled the great evangelist's name (as Gibbon once put it) in ' the decent obscurity of a learned language '—

> Leuconomus (beneath well-sounding Greek
> I slur a name a poet must not speak).

This sort of thing dies uncommonly hard.   There are some delicious examples of it in Victorian literature.

The heroine of *The Angel in the House* was a daughter of Dr. Andrews, who exercised a distinguished ministry for many years at Sutherland Chapel, Camberwell, and who, by the way, was once tutor to John Ruskin. But Coventry Patmore, in the poem, made him a dean. A dignitary of the Established Church, in apron and gaiters, might be permitted to figure in the pages of that sugary epic, against a suitable background of cathedral and cloisters, but an Independent minister— never ! The author evidently felt that there really were limits to the poet's licence, *sunt denique fines*.

There is still another factor in the problem. For it is undoubtedly true that the great events and the great experiences of religion are not altogether patient of purely literary expression. There is real insight in the lines of Boileau—

> De la foi d'un Chrétien les mystères terribles
> D'ornemens égayez ne sont point susceptibles.

Mark Pattison once remarked that this couplet was being disproved in that very age by Milton's great epic. That, however, is a very debatable conclusion. After all, Milton (like Dante) dealt mainly with what may be called the mythology of religion, and it is only that which is generally capable of literary treatment. The supreme facts in the life of our Lord and the profounder moods of the soul's experience can only be adequately described in words which breathe so pure and passionate a spirit of awe and penitence that they scarcely belong to the literature of earth at all—at the most they constitute a small and sacred province of the realm of letters, *hortus conclusus, fons signatus*, where the multitude of men would hardly wish, or dare, to tread. Some of the classical works of devotion and some of the hymns of the Middle Ages, of Pietism, and of Methodism, are undoubtedly great literature, but it is not literature that moves upon the familiar plane or that makes the widest appeal. Novalis and Goethe both belong to literature, but scarcely in the same sense. Charles Wesley has a place in English letters as sure as that of Pope, but it is not the same kind of place. Religious literature, even when it is most absolute, is still a sort of sanctuary, remote and enclosed, amid the wide fields of Castaly.

For the essential character of literature, in the broad sense of the word, is (as Dora Greenwell said with fine discernment), ' a wide Naturalism, which, as it were, finds room within it for all things, not only depicting them, but in some measure delighting in them as they are. Could this genial abandonment co-exist with a deepened moral consciousness, far less, surely, with the simplicity and severity of Christ ? '

That, indeed, is the heart of the problem. It is the business of literature to deal with life in all its wide variety, the life of humanity as it is, the best and the worst of it. But there are many things in the life of the world which religion must denounce, or resent, or challenge, at the least. This conflict of purpose between the moral and the merely literary emerged as early as Plato, and it will be remembered that all but the most austere poetry and music was banished from the *Republic*. When the great purpose of life is deliberately conceived in terms of character, limits are at once imposed upon the enjoyment and use of

literature. The canon of ' art for art's sake ' is forthwith superseded, and the reaction of literature upon
character and conduct becomes the supreme issue.
It is no longer a question merely of interest or beauty,
but a question of what sort of effect such literature is
likely to have upon our moral and spiritual life. This
at once restricts the range and the appreciation of all
imaginative art.

For there is a profound sense in which the world of
literature, as Plato felt, is a world of illusion. It is the
region of εἰκασία, not of ἐπιστήμη. ' What shadows
we are,' said Burke, on a memorable occasion, ' and
what shadows we pursue ! '   Now it is to this world of
shadows that literature is native. Religion and
philosophy, which desire truth at all costs, must seek
to live in a world of light, and there is always an austere
quality in light. The beauty that may dwell in the
light is a pure and heavenly beauty. It is among the
shadows and in the twilight that what is sensuous
and romantic in the world is to be found. ' But I
cannot tell ' (as Bacon writes), ' This same Truth is
a naked and open daylight that doth not shew the
masques and mummeries and triumphs of the world
halfe so stately and daintily as candlelight.' And the
great mass of the world's literature deals with what
are, after all, from the religious standpoint, ' the
masques and mummeries ' of the world—the fashion of
a world that is passing away.

In a word, since literature is largely of this temporal
world, and religion is essentially of the ultimate world
of the spirit, there must be, if not a severance or a
debate, at least a lack of full and final sympathy

between them. The two domains of the mind and of the soul are not yet wholly under one rule, and it is not until the kingdoms of this world are become the kingdom of Christ that the province of letters and the realm of religion will be merged into one indivisible empire.

II
THE GREEK ANTHOLOGY

—— ἔστι δὲ μύσταις
κοινὸς ὁ τῶν Μουσέων ἡδυεπὴς στέφανος.

Meleager.

II

THE GREEK ANTHOLOGY

THE Greek Anthology is in many respects the most astonishing collection of verse in the world. In mere bulk, in the number of writers represented in it, and in the immense stretch of time which it covers, it remains unique. It contains more than four thousand poems, by more than three hundred authors, whose dates range from the seventh century before Christ to the eleventh century of our era. The poems are of almost every genre and on almost every theme ; practically the only characteristic which they all share is brevity.

This brevity is due in the first place to the lapidary origin of the epigram—the word ἐπίγραμμα originally meant an inscription. Now an inscription (whether upon a tomb or a statue or a votive offering) must be short, and that necessary brevity led directly to intellectual restraint. Diffuseness of thought was as impossible as diffuseness of style : an effective ἐπίγραμμα was necessarily the terse expression of a single thought. Then it became established as a literary form, and was used in extended ways. Epigrams were written that were not meant to be engraved, and that had no votive or memorial significance. Almost any brief verse, sententious, humorous, amatory, was classed as an epigram, by virtue of its economy of speech. Now a very large part of the interest of the Anthology lies in this gnomic quality—in the large number of epigrams (in the modern sense of the word) each consisting of a few lines which express some single conception with finality. For the extreme brevity which goes with extreme conciseness is the double quality of the epigram. This is recognized by the epigrammatists themselves, again and again. The proem of Philippus describes his *Garland* as a collection of ὀλιγοστιχία—' do thou, noble Camillus, who knowest the fame of the elder poets, know also *the few-lined verses* of the younger.' And Parmenion, in an epigram on the epigram, says that if one has many lines it does not keep to the law of the Muses, ' for many-circled is the long race, but in the stadion short and sharp is the strain on the runner's breath.' But brevity here is the body rather than the soul of wit. To pursue Parmenion's metaphor the epigram has not merely speed, but the speed that reaches a very definite goal. The essence of the epigram is a species of intellectual precision. It is a swift and penetrating directness that strikes some target of thought in the very centre. It may be a moral truth, or an attractive fancy, or an intriguing parallel between things of the world and things of the spirit; but the essential point is that the thought should be so vividly conceived and so sharply expressed that one is left with a sense of unerring certainty of aim—there is no dubiety or diffuseness either in the thought or in the language, but an austere exactitude that admits neither of question nor of refinement. The thing is uttered shortly, sufficiently, finally.

But the Anthology contains much more than mere

epigrams. It contains epigrammatic verse which
possesses the most absolute lyrical quality. Here the
characteristic of brevity is alone sufficient to raise a
very interesting issue. Edgar Allan Poe said that a
long poem is a paradox, and if his words are rightly
understood we believe that the criticism is wise and
suggestive. That is to say, it is simply impossible even
for a poet of supreme genius to maintain a high level
of inspiration and passion for hundreds of pages together. So that a long poem like an epic becomes in
fact a long piece of versified prose, or prosaic verse,
which only rises in occasional passages into the exalted
mood of real poetry. This is only another way of
saying that real poetry is always lyrical in quality
whatever its setting may be. Since the lyric depends
thus upon a moment of high inspiration, it is natural
that it should find its most frequent expression in a
brief poem, and it is therefore not surprising that the
verse of the Anthology should preserve some of the
finest moments of the Greek lyric. The great charm
of the Anthology therefore lies in a few flawless lyrics,
and in a multitude of finished epigrams ; the second
naturally in much larger numbers than the first, since
wit, though none too common in the world, is found a
good deal more frequently than pure inspiration.

It appears that there had been collections of inscriptions by Philochorus, about 300 B.C., by Polemon
Periegetes, about a century later, and by others at an
early date, but the real beginning of the Anthology
dates from Meleager of Gadara, who is one of the
principal contributors to it. About the year 60 B.C.
Meleager gathered together a collection of epigrammatic

poetry under the title of *The Garland* (Στέφανος), which contained poems by himself and forty-six of his predecessors. The collection appears to have been arranged alphabetically, according to the initial letter of each epigram. Meleager prefixed an introductory poem in which each poet is compared with a flower ; it is in this proem that there is the famous description of the poems of Sappho included in the selection as βαιὰ μέν, ἀλλὰ ῥόδα, ' few, indeed, but roses.'

Later Philippus of Thessalonica made another collection, also called *The Garland*, from the writings of thirteen poets subsequent to Meleager. Still later, in the reign of Hadrian, another collection was made by Diogenianus of Heracleia, and within the same period Strato of Sardis compiled the unhappy collection known as the Μοῦσα Παιδική, which reflects one of the darkest features of Greek life. Much later, again, in the reign of Justinian there was a considerable revival of epigrammatic poetry, and a new collection was made by Agathias of Myrina, with the title of *The Circle* (Κύκλος).

All these, and other collections made later, are now lost, except as they were partially incorporated into a large collecton, in fifteen books, by Constantinus Cephalus, who probably lived in the reign of Constantine Porphyrogenitus, early in the tenth century. A single manuscript of this collection survives. Cephalus seems to have made extracts from the existing collections, with additions from other epigrammatists.

Then another collection was edited by the monk Maximus Planudes, who lived early in the fourteenth century. He was sent by the Emperor Andronicus II as ambassador to Venice, and is remembered as having translated several Latin works into Greek, including some of Augustine's writings. His collection omitted much of what is found in Cephalus, but fortunately preserved the epigrams on works of art ; probably these would otherwise have been lost, since they appear to have been accidentally omitted from the one manuscript of Cephalus that has been preserved.

The Planudean Anthology was the only collection known at the period of the Renaissance. It was first printed by Janus Lascaris at Florence in 1494. The Palatine Anthology is so called from the fact that the only extant manuscript of Cephalus was found in the Palatine Library at Heidelberg. It was discovered and copied by Salmasius, who was a boy of eighteen at the time, in 1606. Salmasius is generally remembered by his *Defensio regia pro Carolo I*, for which he was so severely handled by Milton, but he was a very considerable classical scholar in his day, and a most precocious one, as his discovery of this manuscript is enough to show. It was printed, more than a century and a half later, by Brunck in 1776. There are many modern editions of the whole Anthology, and also of selections from it, and some of the poems have been admirably rendered into English verse, notably by the late Mr. Andrew Lang.

An interesting picture of Greek life in many of its characteristic phases might be gathered out of the poems in the Anthology. Life and death ; war and peace ; wine, women, and song ; the labour of the fisherman and the farmer ; the pageant of the

3

seasons ; the vines, the olives, and the flowers ; sun-
light and moonlight ; rain and snow ; the temples,
the statues, the houses, the harbours ; the rivers,
the mountains, the sea—all are reflected in the Anthology, as the shifting lights of the sky are reflected in
the still waters of a lake.

Thus we are constantly reminded, for example, that
the Greeks were the seafarers of the ancient world.
Matthew Arnold has pictured the indignant merchant
of Tyre who—

> —— saw the merry Grecian coaster come,
> Freighted with amber grapes, and Chian wine,
> Green bursting figs, and tunnies steeped in brine,
> And knew the intruders on his ancient home,
> The young light-hearted masters of the waves.

It was natural that a people who lived on a mainland
with a deeply indented coast-line, and in a group of
neighbouring islands, should early develop into a
seafaring folk. One result is that there exists in the
Greek epigrammatists a sentiment of the sea such as
is not found in any other literature, perhaps, except
English. Some of the poems in the Anthology give
us picturesque details of seafaring in those ancient
days. We read of the tall pines that were felled to
make masts ; of the sails of white canvas filling in the
wind ; of the ship's timbers fastened with bolts of
bronze or iron ; of the lighter vessels made of hides
stretched over a wooden framework ; of the rudders
and anchors and hawsers ; of the oxen that hauled the
ship up on the beach ; of the galley-fire on deck upon a
hearth of stone ; of the flint that every boat carried
in order to kindle fire ; of the coming of the swallows

and the flowers in the spring as the token that the time for voyages had arrived.

Many poems witness of the toll of life taken by the sea, then as in every age ; the price of admiralty, as Rudyard Kipling calls it. Some are merely general warnings of the treachery of the ocean. One of these bids men avoid the sea, and rather busy themselves with the oxen and the plough, if they desire long life. ' For on the land there is length of days, but on the sea it is not easy to find a grey-haired man.' Some are dirges for those lost at sea, and some are meant to be inscribed upon a tomb. One is the lament of a drowned sailor who has been buried on the beach. ' Why did you bury me near the sea, O sailors ? Far from the sea and its noise should be the poor tomb of a shipwrecked man.' Another asks : ' Who art thou, shipwrecked stranger ? Leontichus found thee dead upon the shore, and buried thee in this tomb.' One of the most effective of these epitaphs upon the sea's victims is by Glaucus of Nicopolis :

> Neither this rude stone nor this sand-strewn mound
>   Marks Erasippus' grave ;
> Look where the wide sea washes all around—
>   He sleeps beneath the wave.
>
> His ship became the angry billows' prey,
>   His bleached bones lie below ;
> But where, amid the whitening leagues of spray,
>   Only the sea-gulls know.[1]

There is a quaint humour in many of the epigrams. Some of them manage to convey a delicious note of

[1] Let me confess at this point that I am responsible for all the translations in this volume, whether in prose or in verse.

irony and malice. One which pretends to be an inscription, says that the statue of Apis the pugilist was erected in honour of him ' by his rivals, because he never hurt anybody ! ' Another relates that Charmus ran a race with five competitors, and came in seventh. But how was that possible ? Well, a friend of his, with his cloak on, came along the course to cheer him up, calling out ' Courage, Charmus ! ' and *he* came in sixth. ' If Charmus had only had five more friends he would have come in twelfth ! ' An epigram on the painter Eutychus declares that, though he had many children, he never managed, even amongst them, to get a likeness. There are several gibes against people of small stature. One relates that when Macron, the little man, was asleep, a mouse dragged him by the foot into its hole. There, all unarmed as he was, he valiantly strangled the mouse, and looking up to heaven, cried, ' O Father Zeus, here is a second Heracles ! ' There are also two or three epigrams on people with long noses, which, in view of the characteristic Greek profile, were probably regarded as even more of a peculiarity than they are to-day. One of these runs : ' I say, I can see Nikon's hooked nose approaching : he cannot be far off himself, probably not more than half a mile. If we climb a hill we shall be able to see him, too ! ' Another is on a man who could not blow his nose, because it was longer than his arm, and who did not say $Z\epsilon\hat{v}\ \sigma\hat{\omega}\sigma o\nu$ (as the custom was) when he sneezed, because his nose was so far from his ears that he could not hear the sneeze ! Another humorous epigram turns upon deafness. It relates that a very deaf man went to law with another very deaf man, and it happened that the judge was deafer than either of them. One of them stated that the other owed him five months' rent ; the other retorted that his accuser had ground his corn at night—which was clearly a legal offence, probably because it was done to escape payment of dues. The judge looked at them, and said, ' Well, why should you quarrel ? After all, she is your mother : keep her between you.'

There are several cynical epigrams upon physicians, who seem to come in for their full share of gibes in every age. One relates that Markos the doctor yesterday visited the statue of Zeus : ' Though he is Zeus—and stone at that—the funeral is to-day ! ' Another tells how the very dream of a visit from the doctor was fatal : it is by Lucilius—

> Once sleeping Diophantos dreamt he met
>   Hermogenes the doctor. Though he wore
> By day and night a lucky amulet
>   After that luckless dream he woke no more.

Some of the humorous epigrams have the absurd note of exaggeration and irrelevance that we regard as characteristic of American humour. One says that the speaker had been promised a horse by Olympus, ' but he brought me *a tail*, with a horse, in the last extremity of feebleness, attached to it ! ' Another tells of a foolish man who was being badly bitten by fleas, whereupon he extinguished the lamp and exclaimed triumphantly, ' There ! Now you cannot see me ! '

A great many of the poems in the Anthology are

amatory. Perhaps in nothing else is the contrast between the spirit of the ancient and the modern world more marked. Many of the epigrams on love are of a coarseness that has happily vanished from literature; but, even apart from that, every reader of the Anthology must feel how the whole of the passion and sentiment of love has been purified and exalted since the religion of Christ began to influence humanity. There is none of the disinterestedness of love in the Anthology—the high and spiritual quality that is found in the poets who write of love in modern or even in mediæval times. But though this may be looked for in vain, there is in many of the poems a graceful and sensitive fancy that reminds one of some of our Caroline poets. An epigram which is attributed to Plato turns upon the name Ἀστήρ :

> I look at Stella, and she looks afar ;
> With starlike eyes she gazes at a star.
>
> I wish I might change places with the skies ;
> Then I could watch her with a thousand eyes !

Many of the finest of the poems of love are by Meleager. His Syrian blood gave a passionate touch to his verse that is sometimes lacking in other poets of the Anthology. Too often this degenerates into mere eroticism, but at his best Meleager commands an imaginative grace and a warmth of sentiment that is all his own. One of his poems complains of the dawn :

> O loveless dawn, why this unkind delay ?
>   How slow and sad thy rise
> Since in another's arms and far away
>   My faithless Demo lies !

Ah, swiftly stole the dawn upon our love
When she was mine to kiss—
Too soon the envious daylight from above
Abridged our nightly bliss.

A great many of the epigrams are votive inscriptions.
Promachus the archer dedicates his bow and his quiver
to Phoebus, but not his arrows, for they are in the
hearts of his foes on the field of battle. Potamon the
gardener, having grown rich by his labour, dedicates
his hoe, sickle, and mattock to Priapus. Cinyras
the fisherman dedicates his net to the Nymphs, since
he is now too old to work. Pherenicus the trumpeter,
having quitted the wars and the altars (the trumpet
was used at sacrifices), gives his brazen trumpet to
Athene. Callimenes the scribe, now that his eyes are
failing, dedicates to the Muses his pen-knife, his ruler,
his pumice-stone, and the round piece of lead that
marks the lines on the pages. Xenophon the wine-
bibber dedicates his empty cask to Bacchus, and prays
the god to receive it favourably, for it is all that he
has! Timareta, before her wedding, dedicates to
Artemis her hair-net, her tambourine, her pretty ball,
and her dolls with their dresses. Charicles offers a
goat to Pan, 'a horned and hairy creature to the
horned and hairy-legged god, a leaping beast to the
nimble god, a denizen of the woods to the god of the
forest.' An aged and nameless farmer offers two
oxen made of barley-dough to Demeter, that his real
oxen may live, and that his fields may be full of
sheaves. Many of these were probably real inscriptions
upon real offerings, but we often see the votive epigram
passing into a literary convention, as in a whole series

of epigrams on the theme of Laïs, the famous courtesan, in her old age, dedicating her mirror to Aphrodite. The best of these is attributed to Plato:

> Of old the youthful lovers thronged my door,
>   For I am Laïs, who once ruled all Greece
> By love and laughter; now they come no more—
>   Beauty departs, and love and laughter cease.

> By solemn gift the Paphian goddess has
>   My useless mirror, since—unhappy one!—
> I cannot see myself as once I was,
>   And what I am I will not look upon.

When we remember the amazing perfection of Greek art, and especially sculpture, it is not surprising that many of the epigrams are on statuary. There is a whole series, late in date, on the famous statue of the heifer by Myron, which stood originally in the Agora at Athens, and later was taken to Rome. All these turn upon the wonderful life-likeness of the sculpture, and ring fanciful changes on this theme. One says that 'Myron was looking for his own heifer amongst a herd: he only found it with difficulty by driving off the rest.' Another makes the statue ask a calf why it approaches, lowing, for ' the sculptor put no milk in my udder.' Several others are on the statue of Aphrodite by Praxiteles at Cnidus. One, which is attributed to Plato, says that the Paphian goddess came through the waves to see her own image, and having looked at it, cried: ' Where did Praxiteles see me naked ? ' There are also several epigrams on a famous statue of a Bacchant in Byzantium. One runs : ' Hold fast the Bacchant, stone though she be, lest she leap across the threshold and flee from the temple ! ' Among the most graceful of the epigrams on works of art is one—attributed to Plato the Younger—on a satyr chased upon a silver cup by Diodorus :

> This satyr is not graven on the cup ;
>   He is but charmed into a slumber deep.
> Give him a prod, and you will wake him up—
>   The silver is asleep !

Many of the epigrams are epitaphs. Some are genuine inscriptions, like the famous one by Simonides on the Spartans who fell at Thermopylae : ' Stranger, tell the Lacedaemonians that here we lie obedient to their laws.' Some of these convey a strange sense of pathos across the centuries. A father builds a tomb for his son : it ought to have been the other way round, ' but Envy was swifter than Justice.' The inscription upon the tomb of Baucis the bride tells how she died on her wedding night, and ' her pyre was lighted with the very torches that burned while the Hymenaeal song was sung.' Some touching epitaphs relate to slavery, and more than one witnesses to ' the constant service of the antique world.' Timanthes, a Lydian slave, tells the passer-by from his tomb that he was laid in a freeman's grave by his master, who was his foster-son. ' Live long and prosper, and if, stricken in years, thou comest to me, in Hades also I am thine, O master ! ' Another says that Zosime, ' never a slave but in body, has now found freedom for her body too.' Another is on a

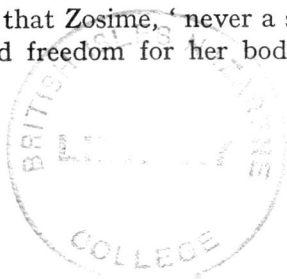

baby-slave who fell from some steps and died of the hurt. 'When he saw his revered master running to him, he stretched out his baby arms. Earth! lie lightly on the little bond-child : be kind to Korax, only two years old.'

Other epigrams are examples of the epitaph passing into a literary convention. Such are probably the two superb epitaphs so superbly translated by Shelley —one of them on Plato, and the other thought to be written by him. Such, too, is the epitaph on Democritus in which the laughing philosopher is commended to the keeping of Pluto that he, 'the ruler of the laughterless people, may have at least one among them who laughs,' and probably other epitaphs which are merely mordant witticisms, like that which says 'I, Dionysius, lie here, sixty years old. I never married : I wish my father never had ! '

There is the characteristic hopelessness of the pagan outlook in many of these poems. 'Naked I came upon the earth, and naked shall I go beneath it. Why do I vainly toil, seeing the end is nakedness ? ' 'We are all kept and fed for Death,' says another epigram, with savage despair, 'like a herd of swine, to be butchered wantonly.' Another, by Callimachus, inquires at the tomb of a philosopher, 'O Charidas, what is there beneath ? ' and the answer comes, 'A vast darkness.' 'And what about return ? ' 'A lie.' 'What of Pluto ? ' 'A myth.' The epigram ends with an obscure joke about the price of oxen in Hades, but there is no doubting the sadness of that πολὺς σκότος. That melancholy note is often sounded, as in an epigram by an unknown writer :

Time, that grey ghost, with silent steps steals by,
And steals away men's breath as silently ;
Himself unseen, he snatches from our sight
Things seen, and things unseen he brings to light.
O life of man ! to what a dubious mark
Do we advance, still marching toward the dark !

There are many epigrams by Christian writers, mostly inscriptions from Byzantine churches : several are by Gregory Nazianzen. It must be confessed that these are the least interesting and the least inspired things in the whole Anthology. Doubtless this is due in part to the date ; the great age of the epigrammatists was past by the time that Christianity had established itself, and these writers were using an archaic medium which had become artificial. Moreover, it is only too evident, from the themes and from the tone of these epigrams, that the spiritual degeneration of the Eastern Church was already far advanced. We cannot resist the conviction, however, that another factor is present, and an important one. The fact is that the spiritual truths of the Christian religion do not lend themselves to this kind of literary expression. For the utterance of evangelical realities a simplicity, a sincerity, a pure and penitential passion are necessary that involve the negation of almost everything in the way of literary artifice. The books of the New Testament and the great classics of devotion have the quality of literature, it is true, but it is literature at its simplest, with scarcely anything of the deliberate art of the man of letters who is consciously writing with an eye upon imaginative effect and verbal music.

And that is precisely what the most effective epigrammatists are doing. The literary art which the Anthology represents is a deliberate and conscious art, for the most part. For that very reason it is perhaps not literature at its greatest, but a great deal of it has nevertheless a singular interest and an imperishable charm.

III
WALTHER VON DER VOGELWEIDE

Her Walther von der Vogelweide,
Swer des vergaez' der taet' mir leide!

Hugo von Trimberg.

III

WALTHER VON DER VOGELWEIDE

THE first thing Heinrich Heine did when he arrived in Paris, in 1831, was to go to the Bibliothèque Nationale, to see a mediæval manuscript, ' the precious sheets which have preserved for us the poems of Walther von der Vogelweide, the greatest of the German lyrists.' All later literary criticism has confirmed Heine's verdict. His own poetic contemporaries freely acknowledged Walther von der Vogelweide as their master, and during the last fifty years, which have witnessed such a remarkable renewal of interest in the lyrical poetry of the Middle Ages, Walther has been acclaimed afresh as the greatest of the Minnesingers. He would have been a great poet in any age, and a few of his lyrics are unquestionably amongst the finest in European literature.

The lyrical movement which is represented by the Troubadours of the South of France and the Minnesingers of the South of Germany is one of the most interesting phenomena in the history of literature. It is difficult to say why there should have been such a poetical renaissance at such a time. Lyrical impulses which defy research visit the spirits of men throughout a country or throughout a continent in the destined age. The wind bloweth where it listeth. A general inspiration must be imagined to account for ' those melodious bursts that fill The spacious times of great Elizabeth.' And some such widespread stirring of the intellectual life must have caused the sudden springtide of poesy which blossomed in the twelfth and thirteenth centuries.

Two or three formative influences may perhaps be discerned. One was the spirit of chivalry. The exalted ideal of personal honour, and personal service on behalf of the oppressed, the devout homage paid to woman, the freer intercourse which became possible through the fact that the knightly order promoted equality—all these contributed to make life more gentle and gracious, and therefore to prepare the way for what used to be finely called ' the humaner letters.' Then there was the unique event of the Crusades. Everything that breaks down national insularity, at least in its more extreme forms, tends to make literature flourish. The fact that multitudes of men had crossed Europe, and had mixed with warriors and priests and pilgrims of other nationalities, and had seen something of ancient and alien civilizations, was in itself an expanding discipline for the mind. The influence of wandering scholars, passing from one university to another, with a tincture of classical learning in their conversation, and something of the lyrical spirit in their students' songs, still further helped to foster that eager minstrelsy of love and nature which is so distinct and delightful an episode in mediæval literature, and which attained its highest point in the lyrics of Walther.

All that the average Englishman knows of Walther is probably derived from one of Longfellow's poems, and from one of Wagner's operas. The fact that Walther wrote in Middle High German is naturally a difficulty. Yet the language is perhaps not more remote from modern German than the diction of Chaucer is from modern English. Moreover, many of Walther's best lyrics are to be found modernized in German anthologies, and of late years many of them have been made accessible to the English reader in scholarly and skilful versions, though probably none realize how utterly hopeless is the task of translation, except those who have attempted it. A nameless charm evaporates in the process. What was delicate, subtle, airy, in the original becomes inevitably stiff and laboured in the version. As the Italians have it, ' Traduttori, traditori' (' Translators are traitors ').

Walther von der Vogelweide was born in the year 1170. The tone of contemporary references witnesses to the fact that he was of gentle birth. He is generally described as ' hêr (Herr) Walther,' which was equivalent to *miles*, Ritter. *Fogilweida* (the Bird Meadow) signifies in Old High German a forest clearing, where birds gathered together. There are many German place-names of similar construction, and they mostly belong to places in the midst of the forests. Walther's first appearance at the Court of Vienna, his friendship with other Minnesingers who belonged to the region, and some peculiarities of dialect, make it probable that he came from the Tyrol. It is almost certain that a hamlet called Vogelweide, lying south of the Brenner, in the Upper Wipthal, was his birthplace.

We find him first as a young minstrel at the brilliant Court of Austria. A famous Minnesinger, Reinmar

4

of Hagenau, was established here, and Walther became his pupil, or, as others will have it, his rival. The younger man must have been both, in a measure, for it is equally certain that he learned much of his art from Reinmar's poems, and that he speedily out-stripped the elder minstrel's renown. One of Walther's poems is dedicated to the memory of Reinmar. The death of Frederick the First, in 1198, scattered the little coterie of minstrels, and Walther went to the Court of Philip of Swabia. He was present, in September, 1198, at Philip's coronation at Mainz. He does not seem to have got on very well with this prince, for he afterwards addressed a poem to him reproving him for niggardliness alike in his gifts and in his thanks, and reminding him of the generosity of Saladin, who said that a King's hand should be like a sieve, and of Richard Cœur de Lion, who was freed from captivity by the payment of such a huge ransom. One may accept the magnanimous Saracen as an exemplar of liberality, but the extortion of a large sum from Richard (or rather from his subjects), as the price of his freedom, is scarcely evidence of generosity on the part of ' Eleanor's undaunted son.'

Later, Walther made a short stay at the Court of Duke Bernhard of Carinthia. Then we find him for some years with the Landgraf of Thuringia, at the famous castle of the Wartburg. Not many places in Europe have associations of such various and vivid interest. Besides its connexion with Walther, the Wartburg was the home of St. Elizabeth of Hungary, the sweetest saint of mediaeval Catholicism, and it was the retreat of Luther after the Diet of Worms, in that

memorable year of seclusion when he translated the
New Testament into German.   Walther describes in a
poem the bustle and the revelries of the Thuringian
Court.   He tells us that you can hardly hear yourself
speak in the general buzz of talk, for the Landgraf
delights in crowds of courtiers, and is so prodigal in his
housekeeping, that if good wine were a thousand
pounds a cask, still his knight's cups would never stand
empty.

Legend makes Walther play a prominent part in the
poetic contest known as the ' War of the Wartburg,'
about 1206.   Hermann, the Landgraf, summoned the
best-known poets of the day to a trial of skill at his
castle.   Amongst them were Wolfram von Eschenbach,
Heinrich von Ofterdingen, Reinmar von Zweter,
Biterolf, The Virtuous Scribe, and Walther.   The
accretion of legend around the ' Sängerkrieg ' makes it
difficult to say exactly what happened.   According to
one narrative the competitors agreed that life should
be forfeited by failure in the contest, and the execu-
tioner attended, rope in hand.   The magician Klingsohr
of Hungary is also brought into the tale, with a prophecy
of the birth of a wondrous child, afterwards known as
St. Elizabeth.   Elizabeth was born about the time of
the ' Wartburgkrieg ';   she was the daughter of
Andrew the Second of Hungary ;   and she became the
wife of the Landgraf Hermann's son,—these facts were
probably the point of departure for this particular
fancy.   Some of the accounts declare that Walther
was the victor in the poetic tournament.   Everyone
will recall Wagner's use of the ' Wartburgkrieg ' in
Tannhäuser.

Walther left Eisenach about 1211. The Landgraf
had joined the party which was attempting, with the
Pope's approval, to give the crown to the prince
afterward known as Frederick the Second. Walther
disapproved of this policy, and joined the Emperor
Otto.

In 1217 he was at the Court of Duke Leopold of
Austria, and remained until the Duke's departure for
the Holy Land. After this he was under the patronage
of the Duke's uncle and then under that of the Patriarch
of Aquileia. Still later we find him in the retinue of
the imperial vicar, Engelbert of Cologne. One of
Walther's poems seems to imply that in these days he
acted as tutor to Henry, the son of the Emperor
Frederick, and found him a very intractable princeling,
as his later history would lead one to expect.

So Walther passed his life, wandering from castle to
castle, and court to court, depending on the fickle
patronage of princes. The only direct reference to
him in contemporary records is a quaint entry in the
travelling accounts of Bishop Wolfger of Passau :
' Walthero cantori de Vogelweide pro pellicio V solidos
longos.' It was at Zeiselmauer near Vienna, and in
the month of November (probably of 1203) that the
good Bishop bought this seasonable gift of a fur coat for
the minstrel. Never, surely, did a prelate lay out
five shillings to better advantage !

The episcopal gift may serve to remind us of what
must strike the most casual student of the Minnesingers—the pathetic intensity with which the changing
seasons are realized. Our civilization has made us
largely indifferent to what Shakespeare calls—' the

penalty of Adam, the seasons' difference.' But in the Middle Ages the long daylight and the genial warmth of the sunshine in the summer, and the darkness and rigorous cold of the winter were facts which entered into the lives of all. The Minnesingers gave a passionate welcome to the spring, with the songs of birds, the budding flowers, and the returning sunshine ; and they dreaded the dark discomfort of the winter as an annual hardship. The solitary benefit that it brought was the sudden repair of the roads in a keen frost, not a small advantage when every road in Europe was a quagmire during a great part of the year. Apart from this, winter was a season of unalloyed discomfort, which men endured as well as they might while they waited with touching eagerness for the spring :

> In summer's sunshine we were gay,
> The birds were singing all the day,
> But now, alas ! the skies are gray.
>
> The frozen snow lies deep where we
> Once gathered flowers in summer's glee ;
> The bird sits shivering on the tree.
>
> The hard ground mocks the bitter sky,
> The peasants curse, the children cry,
> Ah ! would the kindly spring were nigh !
>
> Then to the forest I would go
> Where the birds sing and the flowers grow,
> And there forget the winter's woe.
>
> If winter stayed the whole year through
> I would desert the cold world—ugh !
> And be a monk of Toberlu !

Toberlu was a famous Cistercian Abbey, forty miles or so north of Dresden. We have translated these lines from Walther's 'Vokalspiel,' a poem of five stanzas, each of which is rhymed throughout on one of the vowels—an example of the prosodical ingenuity that marked many of the Minnesingers.

Many of Walther's poems cannot be understood apart from the complex politics of the Empire in that age. The Emperor Henry the Sixth died in September 1197. A few months later Celestine the Fourth, the Pope who had been his antagonist, died, and was succeeded by a Cardinal who took the name of Innocent the Third. The Emperor's heir (afterward Frederick the Second) was a child of three. His uncle, Philip of Swabia, became a claimant to the imperial throne. But the Archbishop of Cologne, and a party among the princes of Germany, offered the throne to Otto, the Count of Poitou, who was supported by the Pope, as well as by his uncle, Richard the First of England. Otto marched upon Aix-la-Chapelle, and was crowned there. A devastating war followed. Walther was a Ghibelline, like Dante. At first he espoused the cause of the Hohenstaufens, and attacked the Pope, who had excommunicated Philip. In the amazing changes which followed, the Minnesinger maintained a certain consistency of attitude. When Philip died by the hand of an assassin at Bamburg, in 1208, he supported Otto, who was speedily excommunicated ; and after the battle of Bouvines, when Frederick succeeded to the throne of the Empire, and fell in his turn under the Pope's displeasure, Walther supported him. All through, he took the side of the Empire and German nationality, against the pretensions of the Holy See. He uses the boldest language

in his denunciations of the Papacy. The Pope is
a wolf among the sheep, rather than the shepherd
of the flock, he is counselled by the devil, he is a new
Judas, and Christendom is in a worse plight in his reign
than when the wizard Gerbert was Pope. Walther's
political poems exercised a widespread influence.
A contemporary writer on the Guelph side accuses
him of leading thousands astray. One of the poems
of this class begins with a lament over the Donation
of Constantine, at which, Walther tells us, an angel
cried a threefold ' Woe ! ' for then deadly poison fell
into the Church. The ' Donation ' is a myth, but
there was real insight in the lament.

Another poem is addressed to the ' money-box,'
which Innocent the Third had ordered to be set up
in all the churches in the year 1213, in order to collect
contributions for a crusade. There can be little
question as to the Pope's sincerity, as one of the
German biographers drily remarks, for he taxed
himself and the cardinals to the extent of one-tenth
of their income, as against the one-fortieth paid by
all other ecclesiastics. Walther, however, declares
that the ' truncus ' has been sent to befool and beggar
the Germans, and that when it has gone back, full,
to the Lateran, little of the money will find its way
to the Holy Land, for little ever escapes from the
hand of a priest.

As his political attitude would suggest, Walther
was a devout patriot. In some pleasant lines the
Minnesinger tells us that he has wandered from the
Elbe to the Rhine, and thence into Hungary, but
nowhere has he seen men so courteous, or ladies so

beautiful, as in his own fatherland.   Here is a version
of one stanza :

> The Germans are a gentle race,
>   And fair is every German maid.
> The traveller's in a parlous case
> Who doubts it ; sure his wits have strayed !
> My country is the gracious home
>   Of virtue, love, and gaiety—
> Whoso would seek these, let him come
>   With us, and live in Germany !

There is the strangest contrast between the airy
lyrics of Walther and his political poems.   The one
belong to a dainty world of fancy, the other to a region
of squalid and strenuous fact.   Here we are among
gay ladies and gallant knights, roses and lilies, night-
ingales and moonlight, garlands and kisses, wine and
song ; there in the midst of turbid politics, flattering
courtiers and mercenary priests, Kaisers and Popes.
Boccaccio made the narrators of the *Decameron*
withdraw from Florence, when the plague was raging,
to a beautiful garden, where they told their light
tales in selfish seclusion.   A world of pestilence without, and a world of pleasant fantasy within !   There
is a like contrast between the fierce polemic of Walther's
political verses and his songs of springtide and youthful
love.

The genius of Walther attained its final expression
in the two unapproachable lyrics *Under der linden* and
Nemt, frouwe, disen kranz.   These poems are marked
by a wonderful simplicity and spontaneity, un-
diminished by their strange metrical intricacy.   *Under
der linden* was first rendered into English by the
eccentric poet Beddoes, in whose version the delicacy

and dexterity of the original have wholly vanished.
The following attempt at that hopeless task at least
retains the metre of the original :

A linden tree
Grows on the heath,
And we sat side by side thereby,
As you may see
There underneath
The tangled grass lies all awry,
From the forest in the vale
(Tantarara !)
Sweetly sang the nightingale.

For I had turned
Into the shade
And suddenly my lover met,
And then I learned
(O Holy Maid !)
What makes me happy even yet.
Did he kiss me ? With a will !
(Tantarara !)
See how red my lips are still !

There he and I
The hours beguiled,
And scattered blossoms on the ground,
The passer by
Looked back, and smiled,
To see the flowers strewn all around,
By the roses still you may
(Tantarara !)
Tell the place where our heads lay.

How he caressed
My heart knows well,
Alas ! I think of it and sigh !
As for the rest—
But none can tell,
For none saw that but he and I
And, it chanced, a little bird
(Tantarara !)
Who will not say a single word !

Nemt, frouwe, disen kranz has hitherto seduced and baffled several English translators. There is a version, strangely free and incomplete, by Edgar Taylor, who was one of the first to introduce the Minnesingers to English readers. We have again retained the original metre—an important matter, where the form is so essential to the charm (however impossible it renders the task of translation)—in the following lines :

' O take this wreath of flowers ! '
  (Thus I besought with eager words a lovely maid,)
' Be ready for the hours
    Of the merry dance, and come with these bright blooms arrayed :
      Had I instead a jewel rare,
        My hands should place it now
        Upon your pallid brow,
      Believe me, fairest of the fair !

' Accept, O maiden shy,
  What I have gladly offered thee, a fragrant wreath,
No better gift have I,
    But there are sweeter flowers upon that distant heath,
      A wealth of blossom scents the air,
        High in the skies of spring
        The gay larks soar and sing,
      Come forth, and we will wander there ! '

She took it with a blush,
  She held the simple chaplet that I gladly gave ;
I saw her pale cheeks flush
    As I have seen red roses where white lilies wave,
      Then to the ground her shy glance fell,
        But I am sure, meanwhile,
        I saw her sweetly smile—
      What more she did, I shall not tell.

Ah ! I had never known
  Such boundless happiness as on that happy day !
The blossoms fluttered down
    From trees above, upon the meadow where we lay

And laughed, and kissed, but scarcely spoke. . . .
—Alas ! all this I dreamed !
The early daylight streamed
Upon my bed, and I awoke.

But how can I forget ?
Whenever merry troops of maidens trip along
I watch them keenly yet,
For one may be the sweet dream-damsel of my song. . . .
Can it be she who dances here ?
—Ah, lady, if you would
Be kind, and lift your hood ?—
Alas ! my garland is not there !

It is possible that Walther went on a crusade in
1228, toward the end of his life.   This was the Emperor
Frederick the Second's crusade, when Jerusalem was
won back for the last time.   The *Crusader's Song*
probably belongs to this period.   We give the sense
of two stanzas :

To-day at last, I live indeed !
What I have long desired, I see ;
The land that has the mightiest meed
Of praise from all humanity !
Now my sinful eyes o'erawed,
See the sacred soil which God
As man with holy footsteps trod.

Through many lands have I gone forth,
And of their glories much could tell,
But this is Queen of all the earth—
What mighty wonders here befell !
Here a Virgin undefiled
In Bethlehem bore a glorious Child,
Is not this a wonder wild ?

The Emperor Frederick bestowed a small fief upon
the poet, probably in the year 1220.   It was in the

neighbourhood of Würzburg, and here Walther spent the last years of his life. He celebrated the King's gift in lines which we may render very literally :

I have my fief ! hear, all the world, at last, I have my fief !
The February frosts no more shall bring my toes to grief,
I need not sue unworthy lords for niggardly relief.
The noble King, the liberal King, has all my wants supplied,
And I shall never lack the summer's air, the winter's fire.
The neighbours know the happy news, and one and all admire
My prosperous looks : no more will they my poverty deride.

He had long desired a settled home. One of his poems laments the uncertainties of his wandering life, and expresses the Minnesinger's longing for a place where he could at last be a host, who had been so long a guest. He died about 1230, probably at Würzburg, and is said to be buried in the cloister garden of the Neumünster. A delightful tradition tells that he left directions in his will for the birds to be fed daily upon his tombstone. Hence Longfellow's familiar poem :

> And he left the monks his treasures,
> Left them all with this behest,
> They should feed the birds at noontide,
> Daily, on his place of rest.

Walther is the master of all the Minnesingers, and the most memorable figure in the literature of mediaeval Germany. He deserves the remembrance desired for him in the naïve couplet of Hugo von Trimberg, which we may paraphrase :

> Sir Walther von der Vogelweid',
> Those who forget him may woe betide !

IV

SOME ELEMENTS OF STYLE

Pol. What do you read, my lord ?
Ham. Words, words, words.

Shakespeare.

IV

SOME ELEMENTS OF STYLE

EVERYONE will recall the amusing scene in the *Pickwick Papers* where Sam Weller reads over to his father the valentine that he has laboriously composed, and discusses with him the relative merits of two impressive words. ' No, it ain't that,' said Sam, ' circumscribed—that's it.' ' That ain't as good a word as circumwented, Sammy,' said Mr. Weller gravely. ' Think not ? ' said Sam. ' Nothing like it,' replied his father. ' But don't you think it means more ? ' inquired Sam. ' Vell, p'raps it is a more tenderer word,' said Mr. Weller, after a few moments' reflection, ' Go on, Sammy.'

Now the elder Mr. Weller, in those profound remarks, managed to summarize almost the whole philosophy of style. He had discovered the important principle that one word is not as good as another word. Almost all that can be said about style is involved in that—one word is more tender, more dignified, more musical, more vigorous, than another, and therefore there is one word which is better fitted than any other for the subtle, sensitive, exact expression of a particular thought. There is such a thing as *le mot juste*, the inevitable word, *the* word. When John Bright made his great speech on the Crimean War, and said : ' The Angel of Death is abroad in the land : you can almost hear the beating of his wings,' it is recorded that Cobden remarked that if he had said ' the *flapping* of his wings ' the speech would have been ruined.   Obviously it would, for the one word suggests the slow, solemn pulse of an angel's pinions, while the other brings to mind an agitated hen in a farmyard.   An example like that is obvious to almost any intelligence, but where the issue is more subtle and the choice more precarious the principle is the same.   As Renan said, *La vérité consiste dans les nuances*, and style, after all, is a matter of truth.   Style is not concerned with that rough and ready statement of truth which is opposed to mere falsity, but with the delicate precision of language which conveys the subtler issues of truth, whether it be in some matter of visible fact, or in a less mundane region of sentiment and imagination.

The subtle choice of words which this involves is naturally complicated by a thousand things.   It is complicated in English, first of all, by the mingled elements of our language.   There is, of course, such a thing as Saxon simplicity, and the style of John Bunyan shews how effective and how beautiful it can be.   But it would probably be true to say that the style of almost every great English writer owes something to the union and contrast and balance of the Latin and the Saxon elements in our speech.   A good style in English is probably, for this very reason, more difficult to achieve and more effective when it is achieved than a good style in any other European language.   For the double strain is obviously a complication, and it is also (despite the laments of fanatics and purists) a genuine enrichment.   The matter is made more intricate and more interesting by the fact that the Latin element in our language has entered it in three different ways, and over a very long stretch of time. There is the deliberate naturalization of Latin words by scholars all through the formative period of the language ; there is the large absorption of Norman-French words in the centuries following the Norman conquest ; and there is the almost continuous stream of modern French words adopted into the language from the seventeenth century onward.   We do not realize how comparatively recent is the entry of many of these last until our attention is called to the fact by a change in meaning or a change in pronunciation, as when we read in Pepys that ' it was mighty well *resented* and approved of,' and so are reminded that the word had only recently entered the language, and retained the sense of *ressentir* ; or when we read in Pope :

> Dreading e'en fools, by flatterers besieged,
> And so *obliging* that he ne'er *obliged*,

and the rhyme recalls to us the fact that the word had been lately borrowed, and still kept its foreign pronunciation.   From generation to generation protests have been made against these invading words, and the main interest of the protests, to-day, is that they date the process of absorption.   Thus Melantha, in Dryden's *Marriage à la Mode*, is always using French words, and the intention of the dramatist is to shew that the practice is ridiculous, but nearly all the words would pass without notice to-day as current colloquial English.[1]   Almost a century later, in one of Hannah

[1] For example, chagrin, embarras, foible, gallant, grimace, reserve, repartee, suite.

5

More's letters there is a series of sentences full of French neologisms, deliberately inserted as a dreadful example of such borrowings, and, if my memory serves, it is scarcely half of them that would strike a casual reader as anything but ordinary English to-day.[1]

But while words borrowed in recent generations seem to be merely absorbed into current English, without retaining anything very distinctive of their own, some of the earlier importations do certainly possess a marked character, derived from the older type of their original language, or from the picturesque centuries in which they came to us first. Thus most words of Norman-French origin seem to have a specially romantic flavour. This is partly due to the fact that many such words are connected with the trappings of chivalry. The knight's *banner* flying from the *battlements* of the *donjon*, or his *pennon* flashing through the *tourney*, while the *heralds* sound their *trumpets* and haughty *damsels* scatter *largesse* to the *peasants*— whenever we think of such scenes all our dominant words are naturally Norman-French. This is not a complete explanation, however, for in the case of doubled words that have come into our language

---

[1] On referring to Mr. R. Brimley Johnson's edition of *The Letters of Hannah More* (pp. 125–126) to refresh my memory (for it is quarter of a century since I saw the passage first), I find that in this instance it is a matter of constructions and not of words, but a good half of them have become more or less naturalized, e.g. ' I found myself here; . . .'; ' the room which gives upon the garden . . .'; ' I made my toilette . . .'; ' of the last perfection . . .'; ' past her first youth . . .'; ' a tissue of impertinences , . .'; ' the women throw themselves at his head. . . .'

directly from Latin and also indirectly through Norman-French there always seems to be more of a poetical and romantic character about the latter. ' Cavalry ' and ' chivalry ' is an example ready to hand, but there are many others—' faction ' and ' fashion,' ' legal ' and ' loyal,' ' potion ' and ' poison,' ' persecute ' and ' pursue,' ' redemption ' and ' ransom,' ' regal ' and ' royal,' ' tradition ' and ' treason.' Does not everyone feel that in each case the first word of the pair is, as a word, the more rigid and technical, and the second word the more graceful and romantic ? One important factor in this is undoubtedly, in the latter class of words, the disappearance of consonants, and the blending of vowels, with the general softening of the word that results. So that here, as elsewhere, it is largely a matter of sound.

On the other hand, words that have come to us direct from Latin have contributed most of the stately element in our language. Doubtless it is always easy for stateliness to degenerate into stiffness, and a Latinized style in English, unless it is in the hands of a master, nearly always becomes stilted and ponderous, as it did with Dr. Johnson, and his numberless imitators in the latter part of the eighteenth century. Then the critic begins to feel that there is some reason for Heine's hard words about Latin : ' It can never belie its origin. It is a language of command for generals ; a language of decree for administrators ; an attorney language for usurers ; a lapidary speech for the stone-hard Roman people.' It is only necessary to recall Virgil and the great Latin hymns of the Middle Ages—wide apart as these are—to correct Heine's rather pettish verdict. But though there is much that is graceful and much that is tender in Latin, there can scarcely be any doubt that it is mainly the majestic element that Latin contributes to the English language. The great seventeenth-century writers are the glorious proof of it. What is most magnificent in Milton and Sir Thomas Browne is due to the use of Latin words. Observe how all that is ornate and resonant in lines like the following depends upon the Latin element :

> Not in the neighbouring moon, as some have dreamed :
> Those *argent* fields more likely *habitants*
> *Translated saints* or middle *spirits* hold,
> Betwixt the *angelical* and *human* kind.

Or, in a prose passage :

' But the *iniquity* of *oblivion* blindly scattereth her poppy, and deals with the *memory* of men without *distinction* to *merit* of *perpetuity*. But the *sufficiency* of Christian *immortality frustrates* all earthly *glory*, and the *quality* of either *state* after death makes a folly of *posthumous memory*.'

It is to be remembered that the Latin element in our speech is mainly an affair of vocabulary and not of syntax. (There are many minor examples of Latin grammatical usage in seventeenth-century writers, as every student of Milton knows ; but nevertheless the statement is broadly true.) We have borrowed words from Latin and from French, but the grammatical structure of our speech is essentially Saxon. The Saxon verbs and prepositions and conjunctions make up the framework of our speech, but words borrowed from other languages enable us to fill up the structural design with material of a greater variety of colour and contour. That is to say, the Latin element is almost wholly (from the point of view of style) a matter of decorative enrichment, and it is in the Saxon basis where all the nervous strength of our language lies. The Latin strain is much more than merely decorative, of course, for we owe to it most of our abstract words, and but for these English would be immensely poorer in its power of expressing thought. But style is concerned with the form of literature rather than with the substance, and for the purposes of style the Latin words in our speech rank as stately ornament.

So that one of the first things which conditions English style is the existence of at least three linguistic strains in our speech, each of which has some special quality of simplicity, romance, or majesty. But those special attributes, however they have been derived, are mainly attributes of sound—they are the qualities (to give a brief and crude analysis) that go with the rigid consonants and resounding polysyllables of Latin, the less numerous and less stubborn consonants and more mingled vowels of Norman-French, and the simpler vowels and monosyllabic words of Saxon-English.

For whatever the source or the history or the gathered associations of words may be, it is never to be forgotten that words are first and last sounds. And some words are beautiful as sounds, apart from their meaning or their history. The legendary old lady whose soul was comforted by the sound of ' that blessed word, Mesopotamia,' is very much in the same case with R. L. Stevenson, who took delight in the name

of the old shipwrecked admiral of the eighteenth
century, Sir Cloudesley Shovel, because it was 'a
mouthful of quaint and sounding syllables.' Many
men of letters have had a like delight in sonorous and
picturesque names. Dr. John Brown has remarked
(in *Horae Subsecivae*) concerning the names of
patriarchs and kings in the Bible that often there is
'a sensation of delight in the mere sound, like the
colours of a butterfly's wing or the shapeless glories
of evening clouds to the eye.' Some few years ago
there was a prolonged correspondence in the literary
columns of a London newspaper on beautiful words,
and there was a striking agreement as to the inherent
beauty of some English vocables. Words like azure,
bereaved, desolate, forlorn, haven, holy, mandatory,
melodious, peace, splendour, welcome, wilderness,
were amongst those quoted as beautiful in themselves,
and most people would surely agree that they are.
Other words again are ugly in themselves, apart from
their meaning or history or literary associations, ugly
as mere sounds. Catalani, the great singer, declared
that English possessed the most beautiful words and
the ugliest word, as sounds, to be found in any language
—the most beautiful being the words, ' no more,' and
the ugliest the word, ' scissors '! The delight of the
great poets in the inherent beauty of words is strikingly
illustrated in the way that they use proper names,
because here, of course, there can be no question of
shades of meaning. The names of the Greek ships
that sailed for Troy, and the names of the Nereids who
came at the cry of Thetis, in the *Iliad* [1]—both passages

[1] ii. 494–759; xviii. 39–49.

imitated by Virgil [1]—are always quoted as the classic examples. Still, they are not nearly so effective (it seems to me) as some other passages where the names are fewer and therefore stand out in all the greater contrast against the texture of the other words, as, to quote examples chosen almost at random:

'Αγαμέμνων,
"Ομματα καὶ κεφαλὴν ἴκελος Διὶ τερπικεραύνῳ,
"Αρεϊ δὲ ζώνην, στέρνον δὲ Ποσειδάωνι.[2]

Praeterea regem non sic Aegyptos et ingens
Lydia, nec populi Parthorum aut Medus Hydaspes
Observant.[3]

And so in many English poets, Milton most of all: ' Busiris and his Memphian chivalry. . . .' ' Or whom Biserta sent from Afric shore, When Charlemain with all his peerage fell by Fontarabbia. . . .' ' Of faery damsels met in forests wide By knights of Logres or of Lyones, Lancelot, or Pelleas, or Pellenore. . . .' ' Ercoco, and the less maritime kings, Mombasa and Quiloa, and Melind. . . .' ' Where the great Vision of the guarded mount, Looks toward Namancos and Bayona's hold. . . .' ' Blind Thamyris and blind Maeonides, And Tiresias and Phineus, prophets old. . . .' ' Hermione and Cadmus, or the god In Epidaurus. . . .' ' Orcus and Ades, and the dreaded name Of Demogorgon.' It is true that Milton, like all learned poets, is naturally allusive, but the most part of all this that has been quoted is plainly mere delight in verbal music, an unaffected pleasure in sonorous names—

[1] *Aeneid*, v. 116–123 ; *Georgics*, iv. 336–347.
[2] *Iliad*, ii. 477–479.
[3] *Georgics*, iv. 210–212.

that is to say, in words as complexes of sound, apart from their meaning.

For a word, while a unit of speech, is a multiple of sound, and the very letters which compose it have each some special character—each possesses some quality of sound that makes it effective for particular purposes, and harmonious or otherwise in combination with other letters, Ausonius called the letters ' the little dark daughters of Cadmus,' *Cadmi nigellae filiae,* and (to pursue the quaint metaphor) one might say that each of the swarthy damsels possesses a voice of her own, gentle, solemn, harsh, or gay. The letter M (probably deriving both its muttering sound and the wavy line of its original graph from the sea) is always in evidence in description of murmurous noises. The letter S (which similarly owes both shape and sound to the snake—*litera serpentina,* as the Latin grammarians called it) is always prominent where the description is of anything sibilant. Hence M (with the related N) and S will nearly always prevail in descriptions of the sea where you are meant to hear the hissing splash of the spray, and the deep murmur of the waves :

> *Spumea semifero sub pectore murmurat unda.*

> No more—no more—no more—
> (Such language holds the solemn sea
> To the sands upon the shore).

So the letter B (with its related labials) and the letter L, which respectively suggest a bubbling and a lapping sound, will always be found together in descriptions of flowing streams—

Labitur, et labetur in omne volubilis aevum.

> I chatter over stony ways
>   In little sharps and trebles,
> I bubble into eddying bays,
>   I babble on the pebbles.

The letter R will always prevail in reproductions of harsh noises :

> *Ipse inter primos correpta dura bipenni*
> *Limina perrumpit.*
>
> > Open fly,
> With impetuous recoil and jarring sound,
> The infernal doors, and on their hinges grate
> Harsh thunder that the lowest bottom shook
> Of Erebus.

But even the effect of single consonants is conditioned by literary associations. Thus there seems to be, in English, a lack of dignity about the letter J, despite the way it occurs in some beautiful words, and notably in several names of jewels. For, as it chances, there are in our language so many words like jam, jingo, joke, jolly, juggler, jumble, and so many nicknames like Joe and Jack and Jerry and Judy, which carry a sense of something cheap or common, or at the least of an undignified familiarity, and this has conveyed a vulgar taint to the initial letter. I think that Archbishop Trench has somewhere lamented that the initial H in Latin and the initial Yod in Hebrew have been so often transliterated by the letter J in English. Probably everyone who has an ear, and gives the matter a moment's thought, will concur in the regret. How much more stately is Hierome than Jerome, and Hierusalem than Jerusalem !---the aspirated forms were once found in English. Imagine Hieropolis and hierophant and hierarchy disguised as Jeropolis and jerophant and jerarchy—the thing is an outrage.

Thus, while the choice of words is mainly a matter of sound, it is always complicated by literary or colloquial associations. A word may have a dignified and beautiful character because it occurs in great passages of literature, and when we hear it there is a faint echo of some fine sentence in our minds, or it may suffer because of some ignoble usage in the ordinary life of men, from which we cannot dissociate it. But even here sound is not out of the reckoning, for the sound of the word had to do with its use in noble passages of poetry or prose, in the first instance, and it is also true that there is a kind of instinct which generally prevents a word of fine sound being colloquially used of mean things.

Thus, to revert to some of the beautiful words already mentioned, how much of the charm of words like *forlorn* and *splendour* is due to associations with our English poets ? . . . ' *Forlorn !* the very word is like a bell to toll me back from thee to my sole self ! ' . . . ' So might I, standing on this pleasant lea, Have glimpses that would make me less *forlorn.*' . . . ' Bright star ! would I were steadfast as thou art, Not in lone *splendour* hung aloft the night. . . .' ' Thou art as Hesperus giving New *splendour* to the dead. . . .'

Thus literary associations and mere sound are often almost inextricably associated in the charm and even in the subtler significance of a word. In the *Life of Tennyson* by his son (of all places in the world) there is a tragic misprint which illustrates this by way of the extraordinary effect produced by the change of a single vowel.[1] Wordsworth's famous lines are quoted thus :

> Breaking the silence of the seas
> Among the furthest Hebrides.

Now the change from *a* to *u* destroys the whole effect of the line. Why ? The answer is perhaps not quite so simple as it looks. It is mainly, no doubt, because the *a* in ' farthest ' conveys a sense of distance by the mere fact that it is a long and open vowel, and to this extent it is merely a matter of sound, but is it not also partly because it associates the word in our minds with ' far ' in a way that ' furthest ' does not ? While ' furthest ' means *ultimus* as much as ' farthest ' does, it lacks both the sound which suggests long distances and also the association with the word which is most commonly used to describe such remoteness, and which itself does possess the appropriate sound. So in numberless cases mere sound and mental association are involved alike, and almost inextricably.

But, precisely as words are simple units of speech, but complex quantities of sound, so sentences, or groups of words, are units of significance, but still more complicated complexes of sound. So a chord in music is a complex of sound, but a musical phrase is a succession of chords, and not a mere succession, but a deliberate arrangement. That is to say (as regards sound alone), there are these two factors in a sentence—first, the words themselves, as words, each being a combination of sounds ; and second, the sentence as a structure of words, the sentence being

[1] On p. 758.

thus a combination of combinations of sounds. Since a word never stands by itself in literature, any more than a chord in music, it is obvious that the musical quality of a single word is conditioned by the presence and the order of every other word in the sentence. Thus a succession of words not in themselves unmusical may be distressing, or a happy combination of words not in themselves especially musical may become a singular harmony. This is naturally easier to illustrate on the side of failure than on that of success. Flaubert is said to have had sleepless nights over the discovery that he had inadvertently written of *une couronne* de *fleurs* d'*oranger*. Rousseau once violated the facts of history to avoid a banal repetition of sound and compared the Roman Senate to an assembly of two hundred kings, because his ear would not allow him to write *trois cents rois*.

But while a mere succession of similar sounds may be distressingly monotonous, a modulated succession of like sounds may be delightful. Thus, nothing is more hateful than alliteration when it is excessive and patent, but probably every fine passage in literature depends upon a sort of masked and modified alliteration—the recurrence of the same sounds, sufficiently interrupted to escape monotony, yet sufficiently recurrent to create a cadence of which we are only half aware.

Almost any great passage of poetry will illustrate this thesis. Take the magnificent lines in which Coleridge apostrophizes Mont Blanc :

O struggling with the darkness all the night,
And visited all night by troops of stars !

On the face of it these lines seem a very unfavourable example for the present purpose, because it is plain that (on the higher side of inspiration and impulse) what makes them great poetry is a quality of lofty and daring imagination, and it might be thought that the musical technique of the lines was a very negligible matter. But it is not, for a brief analysis will show that—disregarding phonetic refinements—half the consonants in the couplet represent practically four sounds, and that one-third of them represent two sounds, while two-thirds of the vowels represent two sounds, artfully set off by another at the beginning and almost immediately before the end. It is, in fact, a little symphony in dentals and sibilants, as far as the consonants are concerned, with alternating groups of two vowels all the way through, and with groups of different vowels, rounder and broader, as an initial and as a penultimate series. Let any one try to substitute other words for *struggling* . . . *darkness* . . . *visited* . . . *troops* . . . *stars* . . . and even if the substituted words are as poetical in themselves, which is not in the least impossible, the harmony will be at once imperilled, and if the proportion of consonants and the order of vowels be much changed, it will be altogether lost. It is true that the lines would not be what they are but for the imaginative quality of the thought, but it is also true that they would not be what they are but for the musical quality of the words, and these are really inseparable, as substance and form are always inseparable in a thing that is alive : they are only to be dissected in a mortuary analysis. 'Grau, teurer Freund, ist alle

Theorie, Und grün des Lebens goldner Baum.' It is where the beauty of the thought and the beauty of the word, that is to say, as regards the principal elements at least, beauty of imagination and beauty of sound, are instinctively and indissolubly fused together in the secret and vital process of the poet's mind that we have great poetry, and nowhere else.

Then when a regular succession of sounds has been established, because it is either musical in itself, or significant in some other way, the sudden intrusion of a new sound, or a new series of sounds, may throw the original series into relief, like a discord in music which emphasizes a harmony. Johnson, in *The Lives of the Poets*, remarked of Pope : ' I have been told that the couplet by which he declared his own ear to be most gratified was this :

> Lo, where Maeotis sleeps, and hardly flows
> The freezing Tanais through a waste of snows.

But the reason of this preference I cannot discover.' The reason, however, like the song the Sirens sang, the name that Achilles assumed when he hid himself among women, is not beyond all conjecture. As Mr. Saintsbury once remarked, ' It is the tribrach that does it.' What pleased Pope was the slow movement of the lines, with their open vowels, which so well represents the sluggish movement of a half-frozen stream—that movement being saved from mere monotony, and at the same time emphasized, by the shorter, quicker syllables of the river's name, as the dull ripple caused by some obstruction interrupts the sluggish flow of the waters around it, and at the same time reveals that sluggishness.

Then, also, since every clause and every sentence must of necessity have an end (and in good writers sooner rather than later), it becomes a matter of importance to secure for every such succession of sounds a satisfying conclusion. It is related in the *Journal des Goncourt* that Gautier once exclaimed : ' What do you think Flaubert said to me the other day ? " It is finished. I have another ten pages to write, but I have got all my phrase-endings " ' (*J'ai toutes mes chutes de phrases*). The method was no doubt fantastic, but the instinct was sound, for an end is even more important than a beginning : it is almost inevitably in the nature of a climax, though it may be a very minor one. This is the justification for that very elementary rule of composition which the schoolmaster defined (and innocently illustrated) when he told his pupils that ' a preposition is a very bad word to end a sentence with.' Why ? Because an unimportant word like a preposition, which does not usually carry any particular emphasis, when it comes at the end, leaves the sentence hanging loose, flabby, dishevelled. Or, to vary the metaphor, the sentence is left standing ajar : it is not closed, as with a turn of the key, or a thrust of the bolt, definitely and decidedly. It has been pointed out how, in the magnificent paragraph from the *Areopagitica*, the effect is greatly increased by the nature of the close. ' I cannot praise a fugitive and cloistered virtue unexercised and unbreathed, that never sallies out and seeks her adversary, but slinks out of the race where that immortal garland is to be run for, not without dust and heat.' A moment's scrutiny will show that the dentals which end the last five words seem to clinch the sentence like repeated blows with a hammer.

Such are some of the main factors, as it appears to us, in the technique of English style. It is true enough, of course, that no one will ever achieve literature by a study and an observance of the laws of style, and it is true that a great writer does not think about those laws when he is writing, any more than an inspired musician thinks of the rules of harmony when he is in the act of composition. But the rules are there, though he observes and illustrates them instinctively. There are canons of style after all, which are not artificial or arbitrary rules, but natural principles—' Those laws of old discovered, not devised, Are nature still, but nature methodized.' And most of them depend primarily upon sound and association.

V

V

JAUFRE RUDEL

Car c'est chose suprême
D'aimer sans qu'on vous aime,
D'aimer toujours, quand même,
        Sans cesse,
D'une amour incertaine,
Plus noble d'être vaine . . .
Et j'aime la lointaine
        Princesse !

                            Rostand.

V

JAUFRE RUDEL

A POET himself, with his name and his strange story
perpetually on the lips of poets in other lands—that is
the singular destiny of Jaufre Rudel.   It is a fate that
any poet might well covet, and that such a poet as
the Troubadour of Blaye would surely have desired.

Very little indeed is known of his life.   The vivid
story that has made him immortal is dismissed by
some modern scholars as a pure legend, and defended by
others as an actual history : whichever it is, we have
only the most meagre details of the Troubadour's life
to add to it.   Apart from the romantic tale there is
little more of Rudel than the shadow of a name.

Jaufre Rudel lived in the twelfth century.   The
dates of his birth and death are quite uncertain ; in
fact the chronology of his life depends upon our
acceptance or otherwise of the famous tradition of
which he is the hero.   If it be substantially true, he
died either on his way to the Second Crusade in 1147,
or, on another interpretation of the story, upon a
second visit to the East about fifteen years afterward.
Some of the authorities who regard the tradition as
baseless would date Rudel's life a little later still.

It should be understood that there is no doubt at
all as to the historic actuality of the man himself.

There are contemporary references which prove the existence of Rudel the Troubadour, and there is not the slightest doubt that the six poems which are all that survive of the writings attributed to him are really his, apart, perhaps, from a dubious line or two which may have been interpolated.

Rudel was of the nobility ; the Provençal biography says that he was ' a very noble man, the Prince of Blaye.' Blaye lies on the Garonne, about twenty miles below Bordeaux. Even in Roman times Blaia had been a place of some importance. In the Middle Ages it was a great port, all the safer because it had a mighty castle to guard it from the pirates. It had been a station on the Roman road from Spain to the Rhine, and for long it retained its importance for travellers by land as well as by sea. Here, in 1160, Henry II of England arranged the betrothal of the infant Richard to the daughter of Raymond of Aragon. Beside the castle, there was a notable church, dedicated to St. Romanus, which was believed to be the burial-place of Roland and Oliver, the famous paladins of Charlemagne. The church, the castle, and more than two hundred houses in Blaye were destroyed in 1683, when Vauban constructed the present fortress.

It is interesting to note that Rudel was almost an English subject. Henry I of England, in pursuance of the policy by which he seized every chance of strengthening his hold upon a rival territory, married his only daughter Matilda, the widow of the Emperor Henry V, to Geoffrey Plantagenet, the eldest son of Count Fulk V of Anjou, who became the father of

a long line of English kings. His son, Henry II of
England, by his marriage with Eleanor of Aquitaine
in 1152, became the ruler of Guienne and Gascony also,
and the land in which Rudel lived remained for some
centuries in actual possession of the English crown.
It is recorded that the Black Prince was welcomed at
Blaye in 1356, after the victory of Poitiers. There
are local and personal details in the poems which accord
perfectly with Rudel's position at Blaye. One of his
sons, *No sap chantar*, for example, has a reference to
passing the Ili, evidently the Isle, a tributary of the
Garonne, which would have to be crossed on the way
to Marseilles, where anyone living in that region
would naturally embark for Palestine. The same
poem ends with a reference to the song itself becoming
speedily known at Quercy by Bertran and the Count of
Toulouse [1]—the reigning Count of Toulouse, Raymond
V (a relative of the Counts of Tripoli, by the way) being
the ruler of Quercy, and having a son of the name of
Bertran.

The one fact of Rudel's life that may be regarded
as practically certain is that he went on the Second
Crusade in 1147—the Crusade preached by St. Bernard.
There are references in his poems that will hardly bear
any other explanation. The eighth stanza of his poem

---

[1] Bos es lo vers, can noi falhi,
e tot so quei es, ben esta,
e sel que de mi l'apenra
gart se, noi falha nil pessi ;
car si l'auzon en Caerci
en Bertrans el coms en Tolza.

> (Stimming, *Der Troubadour Jeffroi Rudel,*
> *sein Leben und seine Werke,* p. 56.)

Quand lo rossinhols et folhos manifestly refers to his taking the Cross [1] :

> The craven who goes not with them
> Who follow God to Bethlehem,
> But seeks his own poor life to save,
> How shall he be accounted brave ?
> Who stays in comfort here at home,
> How shall he to salvation come ?

Moreover, his friend Marcabru, the contemporary Troubadour, addressed a poem to ' Jaufre Rudel, beyond the seas,' and added that he desired ' that the French might have it to cheer their hearts.' [2]

The famous story of Rudel's love, as related by his Provençal biographer, is one of the classical romances of the world. It may be conjecturally amplified, at the beginning, by an interpretation of references in his poems. He appears to have been devoted to some French lady, after the fashion of the time ; but his devotion was not returned. Then, apparently, he went on to idealize his passion, and gave his heart to

---

[1] E qui sai reman delechos
e dieu non sec en Belleen,
non sai, com sia jamais pros,
ni com ja venh' a guerimen.

       (Stimming, p. 43.)

[2] The last stanza of the poem *Cortesamen vuoill comenssar* runs :

Lo vers e. 1 son vuoill enviar
A.n Jaufre Rudel outra mar,
E vuoill que l'aujon li Frances
Per lor coratges alegrar ;
Que Dieus lor o pot perdonar,
O sia pechatz o merces.

   (In J. M. L. Dejeanne's edition of the *Poesies
completes du Troubadour Marcabru*, p. 63.)

the lady of his dreams, much as the English poet addressed his imagined love—' whoe'er she be, That not impossible she That shall command my heart and me.' Then he heard pilgrims who had returned from Antioch talking of the fame, the beauty, and the gentleness of the Countess of Tripoli. Henceforth he gave his heart to this mistress that he had never seen, and spoke of her in his poems. ' He made about her many beautiful songs,' says the biographer, ' with beautiful melodies, and in short verses.[1] He longed so much to see her that he took the Cross and embarked upon the sea. But there befell him in the ship a heavy sickness, so that his companions deemed that he was dead ; nevertheless, they brought him to a hostelry in Tripoli. This was told to the Countess, and she came to his bedside and took him in her arms. Then he knew that it was the Countess, and his senses came back to him and he praised and thanked God who had spared his life until he saw her. And so he died in the arms of the Countess.' The story ends by telling that the Countess had him honourably buried in the Church of the Templars at Tripoli, and that on the same day she became a nun, for sorrow at his death.

There has been an elaborate attempt by modern scholars to discredit the whole story of Rudel's love for the Countess of Tripoli. One suggestion is that it is borrowed from the old romance of Durmart le Galois, where the hero fell in love with a Queen of

---

[1] *paubres motz*, literally, ' poor words,' which Diez regards as probably meaning ' in kurzen Versen.' The point is possibly that Rudel did not affect the obscure style and the involved metres of some of the other Troubadours.

Ireland whose name he did not know, merely upon report of her beauty. Another critical attack, and a more convincing one, argues that the legend of Rudel arose from the allusions in his poems to his distant love, the fact that he went on the Second Crusade, and the probability that he died in Palestine in 1147.

This, of course, is quite a possible theory, but there is no actual evidence against the historicity of the tale ; there is nothing against it, in fact, as it stands, except that to the sceptical mind of a modern savant it does not seem likely that such a perfect romance should actually have come to pass in the world. The story comes, in all probability, from Sain Circ, who was in the neighbourhood of Blaye about fifty years after Rudel's death, so that there was no very long interval in which a circumstantial legend might grow up.

There are other instances among the Troubadours of a minstrel's heart being captivated by an unseen love, and there is nothing incredible in the ideal devotion to an inaccessible mistress, as the great examples of Petrarch and Dante are alone enough to remind us. The one dominant note in Rudel's poems —*l'amour de lonh*—undoubtedly makes for the historicity of the tale. For, as has been acutely remarked, if the troubadour had made such an ado about the lady being far away, and about his doubts as to whether he would ever see her, he would have been merely laughed at if she had been living all the while within the confines of France. There are many examples in those days of lovers who thought little of riding a few hundred miles to see their mistress. ' The distant love ' seems to point undoubtedly to someone across the seas.

There are only two points of any weight in the direct argument against Rudel's story being historical. It is urged that if it had really happened it would have been mentioned in the chronicle of William of Tyre. But the argument from silence is notoriously unsafe. If the thing did happen, the death of a noble pilgrim was not in the same rank as matters of high military and political importance, and may well have been left unrecorded by the chronicler, even if he knew of it. It is also argued that Tripoli was not the usual port for landing pilgrims from the West. This is true enough, but if Rudel chartered his own ship (as he was well enough able to do), he could land where he liked. Moreover, as has been shrewdly pointed out, the mention of Tripoli as the point where he landed, when it was not the usual port, is the very kind of detail that would look improbable to the inventor of a story, and be avoided, whereas if the story is a real history, it may well be correct.[1] The real difficulties about the tale appear when it is asked, Who was the particular Countess of Tripoli beloved by Rudel ? The Provençal biography does not give her name, but legend has always spoken of her as Melisendis. On the other hand, some modern authorities who defend the truth of the story argue that it must have been Odierna. Melisendis was the daughter, and Odierna

[1] The evidence is well summarized in Professor Justin H. Smith's learned and delightful book, *The Troubadours at Home*, ii, pp. 453–459.

was the wife, of Count Raymond I of Tripoli. The
story of this noble house and their dominion over
Tripoli is rather a romantic one. When Raymond,
the Count of Toulouse, arrived in Constantinople in
the early days of the First Crusade, he refused the
oath of fealty to the Greek Emperor which was taken
by Bohemund and the other leaders, and would only
swear to do nothing against the life and honour of the
Emperor. Then, when Antioch was captured in 1097
it was not handed over to the Greeks according to the
sworn agreement, but given to Bohemund, who
indeed appears to have left Italy at the commencement
of the Crusade to carve out for himself a principality
in the East. This was bitterly resented by Raymond,
who had wanted to secure Antioch for himself. The
Emperor Alexius availed himself of the feud between
Bohemund and the Count of Toulouse, and proceeded
to effect an understanding with the latter. Raymond
took the Emperor's part by demanding that Antioch
should be handed over to the Greeks, and he himself
did restore several towns on the Syrian coast which
his troops had occupied. Henceforth the Emperor
and Raymond were close allies ; it was with Greek
help that Tripoli was besieged and captured in 1109,
and apparently it was with the Emperor's sanction that
Raymond's family became the rulers of the place.
Raymond died in 1105, and was succeeded by his
illegitimate son Bertrand, who held Tripoli as a fief
of the kingdom of Jerusalem, with the title of Count.
It was retained by his descendants for several generations. The county of Tripoli was united with the
principality of Antioch in 1200. Finally Tripoli,

which had been for so many years an outpost of the
Latin kingdom of Jerusalem, fell before Kaliwun and
the Mamelukes in 1279. Laodicea, Tyre, Jaffa, and
the other maritime towns soon shared a similar fate,
and, in the stately phrase of Gibbon, 'a mournful
and solitary silence prevailed along the coast which
had so long resounded with the world's debate.'
Melisendis, the daughter of Count Raymond, who is
traditionally associated with Rudel, had been betrothed
at the age of eighteen to the Byzantine Emperor
Manuel Comnenus; but he broke the engagement.
There can be little doubt that this breach of faith helped
to spread the fame of the princess, who does seem to
have been generally renowned for her beauty and her
virtues.

But another opinion is, as we have seen, that the
lady was not Raymond's daughter, but his wife
Odierna. Practically the only evidence on either side
of the question is that while tradition is in favour of
Melisendis, chronology is in favour of Odierna. If
Rudel went to the East in 1147 and died there as
soon as he landed, Melisendis would have been only
about five years old at the time. On the other hand,
if the lady of the story was Odierna (which is possible
enough, according to the notions of those days), the
detail about retiring forthwith to a convent must
surely be apocryphal. She was not in a convent in
1152, but was acting as the guardian of her little son.
This, however, is not absolutely conclusive, for there
are examples of noble ladies, then and later, who had
taken the vows, but were by no means rigorously
confined to the cloister. If the tradition be right, and

the lady was Melisendis, Rudel must have voyaged to the East a second time some fifteen years or so after the Crusade, expressly for the sake of seeing her.

As a Troubadour Rudel belongs to the earliest period of Provençal poetry, which may be dated as the first half of the twelfth century—that is to say, roughly, the fifty years which intervened between the First and Second Crusades.   There can be no doubt that there was a connexion between those amazing expeditions to the East and that remarkable stirring of the human spirit which found expression at this time alike among the Minnesingers of Germany and among the Troubadours of Provence.   The Crusades brought an experience of adventure to multitudes of men ; a wider sight of the world ; an actual contact with strange peoples and strange civilizations ; a closer acquaintance between the noble, the knight, the burgher, and the peasant, in the course of the crowded voyages and the hurly-burly of fighting in a strange land,— all this was in the nature of intellectual stimulus, and doubtless had to do with the rise of that eager minstrelsy which began to make itself heard at the time.

No one would seriously regard Rudel as a great poet, nor even, we take it, as one of the greatest of the Troubadours.   It is true that we have only half a dozen of his lyrics by which to judge him, yet there is nothing very striking about these except the plaintive but monotonous note of ' the distant love.'

The best of the six poems of Rudel's which are extant is undoubtedly that which begins : *Lanquand li jorn son lonc en mai.*   The verses may be rendered thus :

JAUFRE RUDEL

In springtime when the days are long
I listen to the birds' faint song
    Far, far away ;
But soon my wingèd fancies rove
Across the seas to seek my love,
    Far, far away !
And then there comes a wild regret,
Hawthorn and blackbird I forget,
And find that it is winter yet.

Nothing my soul shall ever stir
From this fixed point of love for her,
    Far, far away ;
No lady lives on land or sea
In the wide world, so fair as she,
    Far, far away !
I'd be a slave in Heathenesse
If I could win her least caress,
And still my happy fortune bless.

Troubled and glad, with dauntless pace
I go, until I see her face,
    Far, far away ;
I know not when the day will be
That I her realm at last shall see,
    Far, far away ;
But many a road will lead me there ;
The toilsome way I do not fear,
And God rules all things, far and near.

How glad the moment when we meet
And I am kneeling at her feet,
    Far, far away !
Henceforth, upon that distant strand
(Though I have left a native land
    Far, far away)
I hope to live to my last year,
Sundered no more from one so dear
So distant once, and now so near !

May God upon His heavenly throne
Who gave to me my love for one
    Far, far away,
Of His great bounty grant me this—
That I may meet with her, who is
    Far, far away !
When first I chance to see her face,
Where'er it be, that sight of grace
Will make a palace of the place.

My heart is aching evermore
For one upon a distant shore
    Far, far away !
I pledge my whole life's loyalty
To that incomparable she—
    Far, far away ;
And yet I fear my hope is vain ;
This is my passion and my pain—
I love, but am not loved again.

Alas ! I know my hope is vain !
This is my passion and my pain,
To love, and be not loved again.

A poetic garland might be woven out of the verses
written by great poets on Rudel and his story. Petrarch, who was himself in the line of descent from
the Troubadours of Provence as well as from the
earlier poets of Italy, mentions many of these in the
Trinfo d'Amore. Among the rest he names Rudel,
and tells his story in a couple of lines :

> Giaufré Rudel ch'usò la vela e'l remo
> A cercar la sua morte.

> Geoffrey Rudel, who used both sail and oar
> To go in quest of death.

Heine has a charming poem entitled *Geoffrey Rudel
und Melisand von Tripoli,* which begins :

In dem Schlosse Blaye erblickt man
Die Tapete an den Wänden,
So die Gräfin Tripolis
Einst gestickt mit klugen Händen.

It tells how Melisande wove with her own hands
a wonderful tapestry representing the last scene of
the story—Rudel dying in her arms on the beach—
and how the tapestry still hangs in the castle at Blaye.
In the hours of night, the poet says, the woven figures
come to life, and the Troubadour and his adored
mistress wander about the hall, with many a sweet
speech and many a caress in the moonlight ; but when
the dawn comes they fade away again shyly into the
tapestry on the wall of the chamber. Uhland also
told the story of Rudel in a ballad, but it is hardly
worth mentioning in the same breath as Heine's.

A distinguished French poet has also been attracted
by the story of Rudel, for Rostand's play, *La Princesse
Lointaine*, is a dramatic treatment of it. The play
opens strikingly on the blood-stained deck of a battered
ship that is nearing the coast of Palestine after a
voyage in which the sailors have had to fight with
pirates as well as with the stormy seas. All are
weary and hungry ; Rudel is ill, but he cheers his
dispirited companions with the song he has made about
his love for the unseen Princess :

Car c'est chose divine
D'aimer lorsqu'on devine
Rêve, invente, imagine
    A peine. . . .
Le seul rêve intéresse.
Vivre sans rêve, qu'est-ce ?
Et j'aime la Princesse
    Lointaine !

Then Tripoli is sighted, and Rudel's friend, Bertrand of Allamanon, goes ashore to tell Melisande of the Troubadour's plight. He has to fight his way to the princess through her guards. When he reaches her presence he kneels before her and begins to sing Rudel's song. She completes it, for she has heard it from the lips of pilgrims. Then the princess falls in love with Bertrand in spite of her real devotion to Rudel. He wavers, for he is also in love with her, but he conquers the temptation, and persuades her to visit Rudel, lying sick and helpless on his ship. The dying Troubadour knows her, and is content. She puts her arms round him, and raises him up toward the light of the setting sun : so, looking toward that fading glory, he dies. His sorrowing companions burn the ship, and set out to fight for the Holy Sepulchre.

Swinburne has also told the legend of Rudel in *The Triumph of Time*. The stanzas cannot be said to rank with his best verses :

> There lived a singer in France of old
> By the tideless, dolorous midland sea,
> In a land of sand and ruin and gold
> There shone one woman and none but she.

Everyone knows Browning's *Rudel to the Lady of Tripoli* :

> Dear Pilgrim, art thou for the East indeed ?
> Go !—saying ever as thou dost proceed
> That I, French Rudel, choose for my device
> A sunflower outspread like a sacrifice
> Before its idol. See !

This poem, again, is far from being one of Browning's greatest efforts. Why is it that every poet who has told Rudel's story (except Heine, who only told it, so to speak, in an airy echo) has failed, more or less, with such an exquisite theme ? Perhaps because there is such a pathetic beauty in the story itself that it cannot be better told than in the unadorned prose of the original legend. There are some things so simple and so poignant that they will not endure even the artifice of verse, unless the verse itself be so passionately inspired that it also becomes poignant and simple.

Apart from the fascination of his legend altogether, there is one actual contact, of a really odd and surprising kind, between Rudel and one of our own poets. There is a brief notice of Rudel in Warton's *History of English Poetry*, in the early part of the work, where an account is given of mediaeval minstrelsy, and especially of the minstrels of Richard Cœur-de-Lion ; Warton remarks, in a note, that ' it was Jeffrey, Richard's brother, who patronized Jeffrey Rudel, a famous Troubadour of Provence, who is also celebrated by Petrarch.' He then relates the famous legend, and adds : ' I will endeavour to translate one of the sonnets which he made on his voyage, *Yrat et dolent men partray*, etc. [1] It has some pathos and sentiment. " I should depart pensive, but for this love of mine *so far away* ; for I know not what difficulties I have to encounter, my native land being *so far away*. Thou

[1] This is Nostradamus's reading of the first line of the third stanza of Rudel's *Lanquand li jorn son lonc en mai*. (The better texts read *gauzens* for *dolent*.) The sixteen lines quoted by Nostradamus and translated by Warton are in fact the first four lines of the third, sixth, fifth and second stanzas respectively (in that order) of the poem as given by Stimming in *Der Troubadour Jeffroi Rudel, sein Leben und seine Werke*, pp. 51–53.

7

who hast made all things, and who formed this love
of mine, *so far away*, give me strength of body, and
then I may hope to see this love of mine *so far away*.
Surely my love must be founded on true merit, as I
love one *so far away*! If I am easy for a moment,
yet I feel a thousand pains for her who is *so far away*.
No other love ever touched my heart than this for her
so far away. A fairer than she never touched my
heart, either near *or far away*!'' Every fourth line
ends with *du luench*.' Warton adds, at the end of
his note, *Nostradamus*—i.e. he got his information
from Jean de Nostradamus, who wrote *Les Vies de
plus célèbres Troubadours*.

Now the first volume of Warton's book appeared
in 1774, and Burns manifestly read it. For his poem
Sae Far Awa' is an exact versification of Warton's
prose.[1] The poem was written for Johnson's *Scots
Musical Magazine*, and appeared there in 1796 as No.
449 in the fifth volume. The manuscript is in the
Hastie Collection. Whenever the poem was written,
therefore, it appeared in the last year of Burns's life.
We suppose that no one would regard it as one of the

---

[1] This was pointed out (for the first time, so far as I know) in
a letter to *The Times Literary Supplement* of April 19, 1928, from a
correspondent in New Zealand. It has been found that the actual
quatrains which Burns translated are quoted, in the original, in an
article in the *Gentleman's Magazine* in 1793, written by H. F. Cary,
the translator of Dante. It is signed ' M——s,' i.e. Marcellus, a
pseudonym adopted by Cary in writing to his friend Lister. Cary
is said to have derived the lines from Crescimbeni's *Vite de' più
celebri poeti provenzali*, which is a translation of the work of
Nostradamus. (See *Times Literary Supplement*, September 6 and 27,
1928.) The melody of the song is in Lommatzsch, *Provenzalisches
Liederbuch* (1917), pp. 423–425.

most inspired of Burns's productions, but it has a very special interest because of its origin. A glance will show that it cannot be anything else but a version of Warton's prose rendering :

> O sad and heavy should I part,
>   But for her sake sae far awa' ;
> Unknowing what my way may thwart,
>   My native land sae far awa'.
> Thou that of a' things Maker art,
>   That formed this Fair sae far awa',
> Gi'e body strength, then I'll ne'er start
>   At this my way sae far awa'.
>
> How true is love to pure desert,
>   So love to her, sae far awa' ;
> And nocht can heal my bosom's smart,
>   While, oh ! she is sae far awa'.
> Nane other love, nane other dart,
>   I feel but her's, sae far awa' ;
> But fairer never touched a heart
>   Than her's, the Fair sae far awa'.

To-day Jaufre Rudel is but a dim figure compassed murkily about with the ravage of nearly nine hundred years—like some wraith with pleading hands and wistful eyes that we see for a moment before it fades again into the mists of time.   Yet he is more than that, for this ancient Troubadour has become the living symbol in literature of exalted aspiration and pure constancy, of the romantic love that is cleansed from every fleshly taint, and of all those hopes, undefeated though unfulfilled, that are for ever fixed upon what is afar :

> —— this Rudel, be not looking here
> But to the East—the East !

VI

WESLEY'S JOURNAL

John Wesley's conversation is good, but he is never at leisure. He is always obliged to go at a certain hour. This is very disagreeable to a man who loves to fold his legs and have out his talk, as I do.

Dr. Johnson.

VI

WESLEY'S JOURNAL

It is not too much to claim that, judged by his genius, his character, and his work, John Wesley is the greatest Englishman of his century. Except among his own followers, however, the recognition of this fact has been strangely slow. This is probably due in part to the dislike of evangelical religion which appears in so much of our literature, and which has become almost a convention among historians and men of letters. But it is perhaps also partly due to his biographers. There are numerous lives of Wesley, of varying merit, written by disciples of his, which have not pretended to be literature, and have therefore never made any wide appeal to the *intelligentsia*. There is one biography of Wesley, however—that by Robert Southey —which does more or less belong to English literature and which has been widely read, and it is a very inadequate and very prejudiced account of him. Southey had neither enough spiritual discernment nor enough breadth of general sympathy to write a fair account of a man whose conception of religion was so different from his own, and who was in every way (though Southey does not seem to have known it) so immeasurably greater a man than himself. The final judgement on Southey's book was passed long ago by one of Wesley's old preachers, who said, when he finished reading it : ' Sir, thou hast nothing to draw with, and the well is deep ! '

Wesley was born on June 17, 1703, the fifteenth child of his parents. When he was six years old the Rectory at Epworth was burned down, and the little boy was rescued with difficulty, an event which seems to have left upon his mother the impression that he was marked out for some special destiny. At eleven years of age he was sent to the Charterhouse, the famous school in London. Six years later he went to Christ Church, as a Charterhouse Scholar with £40 a year. He was led to serious thoughts by reading Thomas à Kempis' *Imitatio Christi*, and William Law's *Serious Call*. He was ordained deacon in 1725 and priest in 1726. In that year he was also elected to a Fellowship at Lincoln College. At that period there had gathered around him a few students who, like himself, were making religion the serious concern of their lives ; they studied the Greek Testament together, and were nicknamed the Holy Club. In 1735 John Wesley (accompanied by his brother Charles) went to America, with the purpose of being a missionary to the Indians. He returned three years later, having learned much about the evangelical experience of religion from the Moravians he had met on board ship and in Georgia. On Wednesday, May 24, 1738, the spiritual crisis of John Wesley's life came to pass. He went to the meeting of a religious Society in Aldersgate Street, and as someone was reading Luther's Preface to the Epistle to the Romans, ' at about a quarter to nine o'clock,' Wesley writes, ' I felt my heart strangely warmed. I felt I did trust in Christ, in Christ alone, for salvation, and an assurance was given me, that He had saved me, even me, from the law of sin and death.' Almost immediately after this Wesley and Whitefield began preaching in the fields round about Bristol and London. Many converts were gathered in, religious societies were formed, and the great work of Methodism began, which was to change the face of England.

The main source of our knowledge of Wesley and his work henceforth is the *Journal*, which extends from October 14, 1735, to October 24, 1790. It was published in sections during his lifetime. It does not profess to be more than a record of action, and that ought not to be forgotten, for it is an important limitation in the character of the book. Wesley's *Journal* is not a human document in the same sense as the *Confessions* of St. Augustine or Newman's *Apologia pro vita sua*. It is not a *journal intime*. With the great exception already quoted, it would be true to say that there is scarcely a passage of any personal poignancy anywhere. Wesley does not bare his heart in his *Journal*. It is a record of deeds, rather than one of thoughts and experiences and feelings. Here is a singular proof of this. Charles Wesley died on March 29, 1788. Samuel Bradburn's letter with the sad news was delayed on the way and reached Wesley on April 4. Neither in the *Journal* nor in the Diary is there any mention of the intelligence at all. A fortnight later, at Bolton, Wesley broke into a passion of weeping while giving out the lines of his brother's great hymn : ' My company before is gone, And I am left alone with Thee!' This incident, which alone would be enough to shew how deeply he felt his brother's death, is not hinted at in either the *Journal* or the Diary. He merely records that he preached 'in one of the most elegant houses in the kingdom, and to one of the liveliest congregations,' and praises the singing. It is obvious that in matters of the heart Wesley should never be judged on the strength of what the *Journal* either states or fails to state.

The *Journal* is not only a record of action for the most part, but it is an attenuated record at that. Wesley wrote down in the *Journal*, with a view to publication, a bare outline of his doings. This we are able very largely to supplement to-day, through the remarkable exploit of a departed friend of mine. Wesley kept Diaries which were a much more detailed record of his life than the *Journal*—from which indeed the *Journal* was compiled. These Diaries for the most part have survived. But Wesley wrote them in a kind of cypher—in Byrom's shorthand, with the addition of many abbreviated words in longhand and arbitrary signs of his own. The Diaries were patiently and skilfully deciphered by the late Mr. Curnock, the Editor of the Standard Edition of the *Journal*—a feat without parallel since the decipherment of Pepys' Diary a hundred years ago. Now the deciphered Diaries lend to the *Journal* a new, intimate, and fascinating interest. The record given in the *Journal* is now amplified with all sorts of quaint and vivid details. We can literally trace Wesley's life from hour to hour. We learn exactly what he did from the time he rose in the morning, through the crowded day, to the time

he went to bed at night. We know when he ' shaved,'
' drest,' ' conversed,' ' read prayers,' ' drank tea,'
' writ verses,' ' writ to Charles,' and what sacred hours
were spent ' with my mother.' Many interesting
sidelights upon Wesley's life are found here. The
incessant references in the Diaries to the study of the
Greek Testament, for example, help us to understand
that amazing familiarity with the original text of the
New Testament which is reflected a thousand times in
the hymns and the rest of Wesley's writings. Some
interesting dates and encounters also may be fixed
by references in the Diaries.

The unique interest of the *Journal* may be expressed
in a phrase of Mr. Birrell's—it is ' the most amazing
record of human exertion ever penned or endured.'
It is difficult even for a professed student of Wesley
to realize the astonishing diligence and devotion of
his life, and it is almost impossible to put these characteristics into words. He preached a thousand times
a year, an average of thrice a day, for forty years
together. He travelled about five thousand miles
a year, nearly all of it on horseback, until he was old
and feeble, when some friends provided him with a
coach. Before that he sometimes rode ninety miles
in a single day. He visited Scotland and Ireland on
an average once a year for the last forty years of his
life. He visited almost every town in England scores
of times, and there is scarcely a village in the country
that he did not visit at least once. He was incessantly
travelling, incessantly writing ; and all the while he
was burdened with the anxious oversight of the great
and growing work of God, hampered by debt, plagued

by an unkind and unworthy wife, assailed by innumerable critics, in peril from angry mobs, from stumbling horses, from wild weather; never hurried, never fretful, never despondent, approving himself an ambassador of Christ such as England had never seen before, and has never seen since. Something of this must have dawned upon every reader of the *Journal*, but a close study of it will enormously emphasize our impression of the unexampled activities of Wesley. The text of the *Journal* really minimizes the actual work done. It is only when amplified by the details given in the Diaries, and in the Sermon Register from the Colman Collection, that it enables us to understand all that Wesley really did. Where the *Journal* merely says 'preached,' it often means that he preached on arrival at the place, gave an exposition, which was practically another sermon, when he met the Society, preached at 5 o'clock the next morning, and preached again in the open air before leaving. It is not an exaggeration to say that the work done by Wesley would fill the lives of three or four fairly industrious men. For any man with a conscience, it is at once a rebuke and an inspiration to read the record of these crowded years. His preachers were inured both to hard work and to hardship. But very few of them could stand the life that Wesley lived. Several times a preacher that Wesley took with him as a travelling companion had to leave him after a spell of it, fairly exhausted. Little wonder, either! When he was sixty-one years old, he spent nine hours in the saddle in one day, riding over wild country in Wales, and had nothing to eat between breakfast and seven o'clock at night. When he was sixty-three, he did over seventy miles on horseback in one day, and that a rainy day. When he was sixty-four he rode nearly four hundred and fifty miles in nine days, in very bad weather, amid rain and snow. When he was sixty-eight, he had a rough passage across the Irish Sea, which lasted nearly two days ; but as soon as the boat reached Dublin, he tells us that he landed at the quay and walked straight to the chapel, ' very well (blessed be God), and very hungry.' When he was seventy years of age he received an urgent summons to Bristol : he was at Congleton in Cheshire at the time. He left on Wednesday afternoon, rode to Bristol, settled the business that required his presence there in a couple of hours, rode back to Congleton, and was there by Friday afternoon, having covered two hundred and eighty miles ! In the first week of the year 1785, being then over eighty-one years of age, he spent five consecutive days in begging money for the poor, and succeeded in collecting £200. ' It was hard work, as most of the streets were filled with melting snow, which often lay ankle-deep, so that my feet were steeped in snow-water nearly from morning till evening.' In September, 1786, when he was eighty-three, after a stormy voyage from Holland, which absolutely prostrated his younger companions, he landed at Harwich, rested an hour, and then took chaise for London, but had to stay the night at Colchester, because one of his fellow-travellers was too ill to continue the journey, whereupon Wesley seized the chance of preaching in the town. The next morning he started at five o'clock, reached London before one, transacted business all the afternoon, and preached at night. On August 5, 1787, when he was eighty-four, he left Manchester at midnight for Birmingham, and went on from there to Worcester, Gloucester, Salisbury, and Southampton, arriving at the latter place on Thursday morning. He travelled nearly two hundred and fifty miles in eighty-one hours, with two delays arising from accidents to the coach ; he preached at Birmingham, Gloucester, and Salisbury on the way ; he preached at Southampton at seven o'clock on Thursday evening, and again at six on Friday morning ; and then he went in the afternoon to hear the musical glasses ! On July 11, 1788, when he was eighty-five, he left Sheffield at half-past three in the morning for Derby. About nine o'clock the axle-tree of his chaise broke, and the vehicle overturned. The horses fortunately stood still, while Wesley and his companion crept through the shattered windows. He remarks that the broken glass cut one of his gloves a little, 'but did us no other damage.' He got another chaise, went on to Derby, visited and preached there, and preached again at five the next morning, leaving a few hours afterwards for Nottingham. What a miraculous old man Wesley was ! The world has very seldom seen anything to match this wiry body or his indomitable spirit. Well might his epitaph say that he was ' in labours more abundant, perhaps, than all men since the days of St. Paul.' The year before he died, when he was in his eighty-eighth year, he set out from London in March, and travelled to Bristol, thence to Gloucester, Worcester, and Birming-

ham, through the Black Country and the Potteries
to Manchester and Liverpool, then through Lancashire
and Yorkshire into Scotland, as far as Brechin, then
southward through Glasgow, Dumfries, and Carlisle,
thence through the Dales to Newcastle, down the coast
of Yorkshire to Hull, across the Humber into Lincoln-
shire, then diagonally across England to Bristol again,
thence through Somerset to Devizes and Portsmouth,
then eastward through Rye, Colchester, and Norwich,
and into London once more in October, after an·absence
of seven months. Such a tour would be marvellous
to-day, when assisted by all the speed and comfort
of the railway, for a man who was close on ninety,
especially when you remember all the preaching
and writing he did all through these months, and all
the social intercourse and ecclesiastical administra-
tion that must be added to the total of his activity.
Think of his correspondence alone : it must have been
tremendous. A great number of his letters are extant,
and they are addressed to all sorts and conditions of
people—statesmen, bishops, titled ladies, Methodist
preachers, and friends all over the three kingdoms.
There is a great deal of human interest in this varied
correspondence, and it reflects much light upon
Wesley's own personality. It goes without saying
that Wesley's characteristics, with which we have
become familiar elsewhere, his laconic style, his dry
humour, his unfailing cheerfulness, and his passion
for souls, are all in evidence in these letters, from page
to page.

Wesley was a spiritual director not unworthy to be
compared with Fénelon or St. Francis de Sales. A

wise selection from the letters that give religious coun-
sel of the more intimate kind would make a worthy
pendant to that devotional classic, *A Plain Account of
Christian Perfection*, which, by the way, we take leave
to think one of the very greatest religious books in
the English language. Few men have had such
opportunities as Wesley had of becoming skilled in
spiritual diagnosis, and few men have given spiritual
direction so widely and so well.   Here are some of his
counsels : ' Do not stop one moment " because you
have not felt sorrow enough ! "   Your Friend above
has felt enough of it for you.   " O Lamb of God !
was ever pain, was ever love like Thine ! " '   ' It
may please God to give you the consciousness of His
favour, the conviction that you are accepted through
the Beloved, by almost insensible degrees like the
dawning of the day !   And it is all one how it began, so
you do but walk in the light.   Be this given in an
instant, or by degrees, hold it fast.   Christ is yours ! '
' Those sister graces, lowliness, meekness, resignation,
one would most importunately ask of God, and indeed
without these love is only a name.'   ' Whatever raises
the mind to God is good ; and in the same proportion
as it does this.   Whatever draws the heart from its
centre is evil ; and more or less so as it has more or less
of this effect.'   ' The longer I live the larger allowance
I make for human infirmities.   I exact more from
myself, and less from others.   Go thou and do like-
wise ! '

Next to his matchless industry, what impresses us
most in the *Journal* is Wesley's astonishing vivacity
and versatility.   Surely there never was a greater

medley of interests in any man's life! He talks with all sorts of people about all sorts of things. He is always ready to go a mile or two out of his way to see a fine view, or a famous mansion, or a moving bog, or a disappearing river. He has an appreciative eye for a fine parish church or a ruined abbey. The last remark reminds us that the passage in the *Journal* relating to Cologne Cathedral has puzzled many readers, and has given rise to much foolish comment as to Wesley's indifference to art. He wrote on Wednesday, June 28, 1738 : ' We went to the Cathedral, which is mere heaps upon heaps ; a huge misshapen thing, which has no more of symmetry than of neatness belonging to it.' Now it is true that Wesley was a man of his age, when Gothic was a synonym for barbarous, in architecture as in other things, and it is to his credit that he could appreciate mediaeval architecture at all. He said that Beverley Minster was ' a most beautiful as well as stately building,' and hardly knew whether to admire more the Cathedral at Lincoln or that at York. His contemporary, Smollett, vastly preferred the Assembly Room at York to the Minster, and sagely remarked that ' the external appearance of an old Cathedral cannot but be displeasing to the eye of every man who has any idea of propriety and proportion, even though he may be ignorant of architecture as a science.' This represents the average sentiment of the eighteenth century. Wesley, however, was an exception, and there can be no doubt that he would have admired Cologne Cathedral if he had seen it as we see it. But in 1738 it was an unfinished fragment, disfigured in many ways, and surrounded by a medley

8

of other buildings.   We have seen in the city of Cologne, under the very shadow of the vast minster itself, an eighteenth-century print of the building which amply justifies Wesley's words.   The choir was complete, but half hidden by houses, the walls of the nave had not been carried up to more than half their present height, and were covered by a squat roof of peculiar ugliness ; the transepts were not built, the towers were mere fragments, and, of course, the wonderful spires did not exist.   The fact is that the glorious Cathedral was not completed until 1880.   This is one of the numerous examples in which adverse comments upon Wesley's judgement have been due to sheer lack of knowledge.   The matter is trivial enough, but it is perhaps worth dealing with in some detail because it is typical of many others where Wesley has been harshly judged, because his critics were not sufficiently informed as to the facts of his age.

We are continually impressed by the insatiable curiosity of Wesley's intellect.   He was interested in everything, and that is one of the reasons why the *Journal* is one of the most interesting books in the world. Anything more unlike the fanatic's gloomy aloofness from the world cannot be imagined.   He read all sorts of books, from Sterne's *Sentimental Journey* to Butler's *Analogy*, from Rousseau's *Émile* to Dr. Byrom's *Miscellaneous Poems*.   He was deeply interested in a ghost story, or in a scientific experiment.   He notes, with manifest delight, that he heard the guns of the Tower when he was fifty miles distant.   Another day he took a man who played the German flute to the Tower with him so that he might watch the behaviour of the lions and tigers in the menagerie there under the influence of music—unhappy beasts ! He visits a brass foundry, and notices the bearing of what he sees there upon the language of the Apocalypse. He prescribes a brimstone plaster for pleurisy, and notes the result with satisfaction, and with a gibe at the physicians. He reads Voltaire's *Henriade,* and passes some acute comments upon French poetry and the French language. Something in the day's happenings reminds him of a good story about a sermon or an imposture, and he sets it down forthwith—that remarkable scholar and saint, Thomas Walsh, used to complain that Wesley, with his witty sayings and funny stories, was one of the few men who tempted him to levity. He preaches out of doors at night, and remarks that he has never preached a whole sermon by moonlight before. He visits the prison at Bristol, and writes to the newspapers about the wonderful improvement in the state of affairs there. He reads Franklin's book about ' the electrical fire,' and forecasts wonderful discoveries with regard to electricity in the future. He preaches a charity sermon and collects money to clothe the wretched French prisoners at Knowle. The old man of eighty-seven relates with obvious pleasure that he saw at Northwich a Newfoundland dog and a raven which had become such attached friends that the bird had learned to bark exactly like the dog, and had repeatedly been observed to save up bones for him during his absence ! A few months later Wesley records that a man born without arms came to breakfast with him at Ditcheat, and he describes to us how the poor fellow held his cup with one foot, and his toast with the other. Still a little later Wesley went to Bristol Fair to see 'a monster' (probably a sloth-bear) with 'a horrible roar, between that of a lion and of a bull.' These instances are trivial enough, but they illustrate a steady characteristic of Wesley's intellect. He was always willing to take a little trouble, and to go a little out of his way to inspect anything remarkable. This curiosity and candour of intellect accounts for a good deal.

It accounts for one thing which has been advanced against Wesley from the days of Southey onward— the charge of credulity. That charge, based upon Wesley's belief in witchcraft and apparitions, was more effective two or three generations back than it is now. Then most men dismissed every story of an apparition or a *Poltergeist* as 'popular superstition' or 'credulity.' But an age familiar with the work of the Psychical Research Society cannot be quite so sceptical and supercilious. The very things which, when Wesley investigated and recorded them, brought upon him the charge of 'credulity' are to-day being most carefully investigated and most elaborately recorded by grave men of science. Wesley's attitude in this matter has always seemed to us to be thoroughly scientific and modern. As a rule he does not dog-matise, but merely records with care what he is unable either to deny or to explain. Only recently we happened upon a letter written by F. W. H. Myers to Dr. Gregory some thirty years ago, in which the author of *Human Personality and its Survival* takes this view of Wesley's attitude : ' Wesley and Dr. Johnson, certainly two of the " stoutest hearts and strongest heads " of their time, were almost unique in their readiness to take real trouble to get first-hand evidence as to these strange and scattered indications of an unseen world. Wesley's interviews with Elizabeth Hobson, for instance, were undertaken in a calm, careful, and exact temper.'

He was singularly modern, in fact, in all sorts of ways. In a bewigged age he wore his own hair, and he used shorthand when it was quite a novelty. He was a pioneer in the production of cheap literature. He devised and used before anyone else some of the social adjuncts of religious work which are familiar to-day. He was probably the first Englishman to possess a literary knowledge of German, and we owe to that fact his magnificent translations of some of the finest hymns of the Pietists and Moravians.

The general impression that the *Journal* leaves upon the mind is that of a man of wide interests, with a singularly clear and candid intellect, which was marked also by a restless curiosity ; a man who lived a life of amazing industry, solely dedicated to one great purpose. His temperament was naturally calm—he used to say that he needed heat rather than light—and yet there burned in his heart, with a still intensity, a very flame of love for God and for men. We find the old man resolving, at the beginning of one Diary, late in life, ' *Deo juvante*, to pray every hour, seriously, deliberately, fervently.' There was a deep passion of devotional life beneath all Wesley's astonishing activity. Nothing less will account for his strenuous and sacrificial life—a life which was

one long fulfilment of the prayer expressed in his
brother's lines :

> My talents, gifts, and graces, Lord,
>   Into Thy blessèd hands receive ;
> And let me live to preach Thy word,
>   And let me to Thy glory live ;
> My every sacred moment spend
> In publishing the sinner's Friend.

VII

THÉOPHILE GAUTIER

Tu fus surtout un Grec, et tu contemples
De tes yeux immortels
Les purs profils harmonieux des temples
Dans les bleus archipels.

                          Théodore de Banville.

VII

THÉOPHILE GAUTIER

THÉOPHILE GAUTIER is eminent among French writers
for the very qualities which distinguish the literature
of France among the literatures of Europe. These are
attributes which it is much easier to recognize than to
define, but amongst them is certainly to be found a
remarkable fusion of intellectual lucidity and imaginative grace, accompanied by an admirable deftness
of literary workmanship. Intelligence, interest, a
sprightly fancy, an adroit irony, graceful scholarship,
a delicate sense of style—these are characteristically
French gifts, and there is no writer who possesses
them more completely than Gautier. There are still
greater gifts that he does not possess. He has generally
little sense of the profound pathos of life ; he is not
burdened with the weight of all this unintelligible
world ; he never feels any religious emotion ; he never
betrays any moral enthusiasm ; he is content to dwell
on the decorative surface of nature and of civilization.
But if we are willing to take him as he is we shall find
that there is no more delightful companion in all the
realm of letters. Like Scott (as Lockhart's correspondent said) he is ' such a friendly writer.'

He was born in 1811, and as a little boy must have
heard the reverberations of the battle of Waterloo.
He died in 1872, distressed by the triumph of Germany

and the wild excesses of the Commune.   The place of his birth happened to be Tarbes, in Languedoc, where his father held an appointment ; but soon afterward his parents removed to Paris, where they belonged, and the poet's whole life was spent there.   He was educated at the Lycée Louis-le-Grand, and later at the Collége Charlemagne.   At first, as a boarder, he suffered extremely, for the *lycées* of those days, as his biographer has remarked, combined the hardships of a monastery, a barracks, and a prison.   Later, as an *externe*, and studying under the direction of his scholarly father, he was happy.

When he left college he was determined to be a painter, and he spent a couple of years in the *atelier* of Rioult.   It was while he was here that he made the acquaintance of Sainte-Beuve, the famous critic, who was astonished by the remarkable knowledge of the French Renaissance poets shewn by this lad of eighteen.   Either Sainte-Beuve or Gérard de Nerval (whose friendship Gautier had gained at college) introduced him to the notice of Victor Hugo, who became his literary hero.   About this time he was definitely launched on a literary career.

It was a remarkable period, for it witnessed the romantic revival in French literature.   It would take us too far afield if we attempted to trace the sources of that movement ;   roughly, it was the influence of Goethe and Heine in Germany, and of Scott and Byron in England, that was making itself felt among the younger writers of France.   The romantic movement was a revolt against literary conventions that had grown rigid—especially against the chilly classicism of the eighteenth century ; a return to nature, though not in Wordsworth's sense ; a spirit of liberty and adventure in the realm of letters ; a new sense of the infinite charm and colour and movement of life.

The crucial date of the movement was February 25, 1830, when Victor Hugo's *Hernani* was produced at the Théâtre Français. Both the classical and the romantic factions made it the occasion of a demonstration. Half a dozen tickets were taken to Rioult's studio. ' You will answer for your friends ? ' said the messenger to Gautier. ' By the skull from which Byron drank at Newstead Abbey,' was the response, ' I will answer for them ! ' The reply was a characteristic extravagance. The early romantics rather affected skulls, and indeed anything that suggested vaults, mortality, melancholy, the mouldering past, the Middle Ages—all of which were supposed to be the special properties of a grotesque and Gothic taste, as opposed to the frigidities of classicism. When Scott, as a young man, was translating Bürger, he ' wished to heaven that he had a skull and cross-bones ' !

Hernani was a huge success. Gautier was prominent, on the night of the production, in a crimson waistcoat. He must have made a striking figure, habited in this fashion, with his powerful frame and his flowing locks. His *gilet rouge* became famous ; it was remembered for long as the oriflamme of romanticism.

About this time Gautier published his first volume of poems, soon followed by a second and a third, and his first novel. A little later he joined the staff of *La Presse* as dramatic and art critic. Twenty years afterward he left *La Presse* for *Le Moniteur Universel*.

This was afterward replaced by the *Journal Officiel*. Gautier continued this work until his death, and indeed made most of his living by it. He often lamented his fate, and girded at the hard necessity that kept him at work on his feuilleton every week except for an occasional holiday : ' Jusqu'à lundi je suis mon maître. Au diable, chefs-d'œuvre mort-nés ! ' Yet it may be doubted if any other life would have suited him so well ; certainly no other would have ministered so richly to his special instincts as a lover of art and letters. It kept him in constant contact with the drama, the art, and the intellectual life of Paris generally for nearly forty years.

Apart from his travels there is not much incident in Gautier's life. He had no interest in politics, and, unlike Hugo, was quite content with the Second Empire. Nevertheless, he nearly got into trouble on one occasion. On the publication, in 1855, of a volume which contained the fantasy *Une Larme de Diable*, the Government suspected an allusion, in one passage, to December 2, and the perjury of Napoleon III. It is the passage where the Almighty says : ' The doom is irrevocable ; I am not to be forsworn like an earthly king.' Gautier was able to prove that the story had first appeared in 1839, in the reign of Louis Philippe, and the matter dropped, much to his satisfaction, for he was not at all the stuff of which martyrs are made.

It is all the more to his credit, therefore, that in another connexion he proved his intellectual probity rather strikingly. On the occasion of the Exposition Universelle of 1867 Gautier was commissioned by the Ministre de l'Instruction Publique to write an account of the progress of French poetry since 1848. Now Victor Hugo was the greatest figure in that generation of French poets, and Victor Hugo was the author of *Les Châtiments*, the bitter satirist of ' Napoléon le Petit,' and anathema to the Government. Gautier, like an honest man, wrote enthusiastically of Hugo, and does not seem to have suffered for it. The *rapport* was afterward embodied in Gautier's *Histoire du Romantisme*.

He was thrice proposed for the Academy, but never elected. The names of those who were elected on those three occasions, when contrasted with the name of Gautier, are enough to show the futility of the whole business of an Academy—they were Gratry, Autran, and Barbier. But Gautier was in excellent company in his exclusion from the number of the immortal Forty. If he was not an Academician, neither was Molière, nor Pascal, nor Balzac.

Physically, Gautier was robust. It is said that he ordinarily consumed five pounds of mutton and three bottles of wine in the course of the day. Once, at a fair, he struck a blow of over five hundred pounds on the *tête de Turc*—the popular dynamometer—and he declared that it was the proudest action of his life. It is curious that sturdy men of a vigorous habit are often the most humane in their outlook upon life, and the most subtle, delicate, and fastidious in their artistic work ; and that it is usually the physical weaklings who yell for carnage, who disregard the decencies of literature, and who generally seek to draw attention to themselves by violence and blasphemy. Along with his burly frame, Gautier had one mental gift (as distinguished from his genius) that must have helped him enormously in his life of literary toil—he had a memory like Macaulay's. He once recited to some friends more than a hundred stanzas of Hugo's *Légende des Siècles*, which had just appeared. They found, to their amazement, that he had merely read the poem over once while at breakfast that morning.

Gautier was an extremely various and voluminous author. There cannot be many things in the visible world about which he did not say something (and generally something wise, memorable, and urbane) in the sixty volumes he wrote. But his principal achievement is fourfold—he was a novelist, a critic, a traveller, and a poet. In each of these departments he wrote some of the best things that have ever been written in French. We suspect that Gautier's fame has suffered somewhat by reason of this very versatility. The world will not believe that a man can do more than one thing well ; it insists on his being a specialist, restricted to one line of activity. If a man is naturally versatile, he always runs the risk of being classed as a dilettante ; because he does many things, the public cannot conceive that he does any of them with supreme excellence.

Gautier was, in the first place, a considerable writer of fiction, more successful in his short stories than in his long novels.

Mademoiselle de Maupin, his most notorious novel, might have been dismissed by this time as merely a juvenile attempt to shock the bourgeoisie if it had not been for the famous preface, which seriously sets up the doctrine of art for art's sake, and has become the *credo* of the literary neopagans. The book raises the whole question of the relation between morality and literature. It must be admitted that the moral and the artistic do not merely coincide. There is great literature that is more or less in conflict with the dictates of morality. On the other hand, it is equally certain that the greatest literature of all must have a moral basis and a moral sanction. The motive of Gautier's novel is sexual, in an unusual and unpleasant fashion. Now the ethically abnormal can only be treated successfully in literature in two ways. One is a frank paganism where the moral aspect is completely and cheerfully disregarded, the method of Boccaccio. The other is a method with which we are more familiar in modern fiction, as the names of Nathaniel Hawthorne and Thomas Hardy are enough to remind anyone, where elemental passion and perverse circumstance drive men into moral disaster, and where the cloud of retribution hangs over all. A method which is less irresponsible than the one, and less earnest than the other—like that of Gautier here— is foredoomed to failure. From the point of view of literature alone, the book should have been either more of an erotic comedy or more of a passionate tragedy. To put it in another way, either the moral interests at stake are too serious, or the structural development of the narrative is too slight.

Le Capitaine Fracasse, the other of Gautier's long novels which is best known, is of another type altogether. It is a picaresque story of the most readable sort. From the fine description of the ruined château at the beginning of the book to the happy ending, with the marriage at Vallombreuse, it is a thoroughly innocent and interesting tale. We follow with a pleasant zest the adventures of the strolling players as they wander about the picturesque France of a bygone century. Gautier borrowed a good deal of the material of the book from Scarron, in much the same way as Charles Reade, in his greatest romance, borrowed from Erasmus. There is no serious purpose in the book ; it is merely pleasant romance in the familiar key of *manteau et épée*. It is interesting to know that Gautier began it, dropped it, and then, after an interval of twenty-five years, resumed and finished it. It has the interest of Dumas, with more refinement of manner, and more plausibility of construction, though without the intoxicating energy of the author of *Les Trois Mousquetaires*.

There are few writers who have had a more un-questioned mastery of the short story than Gautier. It is amazing how he manages to convey the atmosphere of eighteenth-century Paris in *Jean et Jeannette*, and of nineteenth-century Madrid in *Militona ;* of ancient Egypt in *Une Nuit de Cléopatre ;* and of classical Greece in *La Chaîne d'Or*. The archaeology may not be faultless in these last (though Gautier was quite a scholarly man of letters), but, however that may be, he certainly has a wonderful knack of suggesting the scene of ancient life as the background of the tale. It is equally astonishing that he should be able to achieve in *La Morte Amoureuse* somewhat of the crepuscular horror that was the speciality of Edgar Allan Poe, and in the little story of *L'Enfant aux Souliers de Pain* a simplicity and a naïve pathos that seem to belong by right to Hans Andersen.

Some of Gautier's best work as a critic is found in *Trois Grotesques*, the volume in which he rehabilitated three writers then almost entirely forgotten—François Villon, Cyrano de Bergerac, and Paul Scarron. Apart from that volume Rostand's most famous play, and one of Stevenson's delightful essays, as well as the most vivid of his short stories, would never have been written. Everyone to-day can quote Villon's *Mais où sont les neiges d'antan ?* and everyone is familiar with Cyrano's astonishing feature, *ce nez invraisemblable ;* and if Scarron does not quite share their resuscitated fame, at least we all know that Gautier himself was indebted to the *Roman comique* for the idea, and some of the material, of *Le Capitaine Fracasse.*

Hazlitt once remarked that Coleridge ' somehow always contrived to prefer the unknown to the known.' Gautier was always happy in dealing with the less renowned writers, and he could give some excellent reasons for his pleasure. ' It is a charming and curious study,' he writes, ' that of the second-rate poets. In the first place, since they are less known, you are all the more likely to make surprising discoveries ; moreover, there is not at hand a ready-made criticism on every striking word ; one is delivered from the necessity of going into conventional ecstasies, and is not compelled to rave and stamp at some particular passages, as is absolutely indispensable with the poets who have become classic ! '

But apart from the success of the book in its main purpose, as an *exhumation littéraire*, it is full of the shrewdest and wittiest criticism, expressed in the most delightful style. How suggestive this is with regard

9

to the literature of France in general! 'Since Panurge's sheep, and indeed before, France is supremely the land of imitation, for the French, so bold on the field of battle and in perilous situations, are extremely timid on paper. This nation, which observers call extravagant and light-minded, has always preserved a profound respect for rules, and has never run many hazards in literature. When they get a pen into their hands the French (otherwise so temerarious) are full of hesitation and anxiety; they tremble lest they should say something new which cannot be found in authors of the best repute. . . . It is only in France that the word *original*, applied to an individual, is almost a term of reproach. Every Frenchman who writes is burdened by the fear of ridicule, and the result is that when a style or a mode has been accepted by the public, all the authors adopt it, happy to be able to decline the responsibility of having a manner of their own. . . . Because of this, our literature is poorer than any other in eccentric works; the general tone is to be found fixed in the majority of contemporary writers, and every period has its particular note of style, imposed, first of all, by some literary success.' That is strikingly true of a great deal of French literature; if it is less true to-day than it was when Gautier wrote those words, the change is largely due to Gautier himself.

How well the following passage, again, describes the frigid style of the eighteenth century! 'Good taste is a fine thing, but it should not be abused; because of it you may deprive yourself of a multitude of subjects, of details, of images, of expressions, that have in them the savour of life. . . . The influence of Louis XIV upon the literature and art of his time was not always happy. They were dominated too much by the peruke of *le grand Roi*. Nature was almost expelled by majesty, by etiquette, by convention. Everywhere a cold regularity was substituted for the charming disorder of life. . . . Poetry always wore a gala dress, with a page to carry her train, lest she should catch her feet in her skirts of gold brocade as she mounted the marble stairs of Versailles. . . . The result was an art magnificent, grandiose, serious, but, with two or three splendid exceptions, rather wearisome.' A criticism of admirable justice, and very picturesquely expressed.

Though he lived all his life in Paris, except for a few months of infancy, Gautier liked to think that he was temperamentally of the South. ' J'ai gardé,' he said, ' un fonds méridional.' It is stated that his family hailed originally from Provence. There is certainly a wonderful sense of warmth and colour in his writings ; his invocations of the sunshine and the summer remind one of the Troubadours. His travels were mainly in sunny lands—Spain, Italy, and the East. The one exception is Russia, and there his preoccupation with light and colour is remarkable. Thus he describes a sleigh-ride across ' an immaculate immensity of sparkling snow, that strange soil which by its silvery tint reminds you of a journey in the moon, through an atmosphere quick, cutting, cold as steel, where nothing can corrupt, not even death itself ! ' Many of his Russian descriptions are wonderful studies in opalescent light and the blanched hues of the wintry landscape that remind one of his poem, *Symphonie en Blanc Majeur*, where he glances from one paleness to another—the snows of Norway, the swans of the Rhine ; the white satin, the white lace, the white shoulders of fair ladies ; marble, ivory ; white butterflies, the white blossom of the hawthorn, the white foam of the sea. In this connexion it is very significant that Gautier's first ambition was to be a painter, for he was essentially an artist in letters. One of the most striking things about his writings, both in prose and verse, is this decorative quality. His astonishing sense of colour is everywhere in evidence. ' Three things please me,' says a character in one of his novels (and it was assuredly true of himself), ' gold, marble, and purple ; splendour, solidity, colour.' This feeling for colour lends a peculiar charm to his records of travel. It reveals itself in many quaint touches. On his way to Russia, for example, as he records his impressions of Hamburg, he notes with enthusiasm the scarlet tunics of the postmen, and laments ' that we rarely see anything red in our modern civilization, which is so much given to neutral tints that it seems ambitious to render the art of painting impossible ! '

All his books of travel are delightful reading, the *Voyage en Espagne* particularly, but the best of them all, in our judgment, is the *Voyage en Italie*. Most of the volume is devoted to Venice, which he loved with a discerning passion, and described better than Ruskin. No one who has read Gautier and seen Venice can ever dissociate him from the place. We see again the sights of that dream-like city as we read his vivid pages. What wonderful vignettes he often gives in a sentence or two! Who can forget the description of his first passage down the Grand Canal in the darkness, 'when every gondola gliding noiselessly along seemed to hide a pair of lovers, or a corpse with a dagger thrust into its breast'? Or the brilliant paragraphs in which he rhapsodizes about St. Mark's, with its 'aspect of a temple, a basilica, and a mosque; that strange and mysterious edifice, at once exquisite and barbarous; that immense accumulation of riches; that pirates' church, made of fragments gained by robbery or conquest from all the civilizations; that Oriental dream, petrified by the power of an enchanter; a Moorish church or a Christian mosque, built by a converted Caliph; that collection of columns, of capitals, of sculptures, of enamels, of mosaics; that mixture of styles, Greek, Roman, Byzantine, Arabic, Gothic, which yet produces an entire effect of perfect harmony; that golden cavern, encrusted with gems, splendid and sombre, at once sparkling and mysterious!'

No one who has read those pages will forget them if he has ever seen the pigeons flying around the Campanile. And everybody who has ever 'swum in a gondola' (in Shakespeare's phrase) will remember Gautier's words about the Grand Canal. 'Every piece of wall recalls a history; every house is a palace; every palace is both a masterpiece and a legend. At every stroke of the gondolier's oar you quote a name which was as well known at the time of the Crusades as it is to-day. The Grand Canal is an immense gallery, open to the skies, where you may study from your seat in the gondola the art of seven or eight centuries.'

The style of Gautier is masterly, both in prose and in verse, and perhaps nothing is more masterly than the difference between the one and the other. His poetry is almost the last word in chastity of form, in minute delicacy, in disciplined and scholarly grace. His prose is not less artistic, but it is naturally freer, more varied, more picturesque, with a quaint allusiveness and an abundance of graceful images. He was very widely read, and his vocabulary is remarkably rich. It is said that dictionaries were amongst his favourite reading, and one can well believe it. He rejoiced over a vivid and unusual word as over hid treasure, and when once he had found it he used it with an infallible felicity. No man ever had a keener sense of what he himself called *la réjouissante bizarrerie des mots*. His fanciful metaphors are a continual delight, as when he describes the trellised vines of Mestre ' reaching out hands to one another, as if to dance an immense farandole around the field,' and when he compares the dark cupola of San Simeone Piccolo, among the silvery domes of Venice, with ' the black armour of the mysterious knight in the tourneys of the Middle Ages.' When he is in Belgium, the locomotive of his train ' whistles like an asthmatic whale,' and when he is in Russia a horse, heated by a gallop in that bitter atmosphere, ' breathes out jets of smoke, like a dragon in a fairy tale.' Many of his most casual remarks have a quality of admirable observation, as when passing the quays of the Spree in Berlin, he notes that ' vessels on a river or a canal in the middle of a city always have a charming effect.' What a force and finality there is, too, in some of his single phrases, as when, condemning the furious ornamentation of some of the Jesuit churches, he declares that it looks ' like sickly excrescences upon diseased stone ' !

The greatest work of Gautier, however, is to be found in his poetry, and especially in the volume of verse entitled *Émaux et Camées*. The title is apt. Every poem in the book has the delicate grace of a cameo, the finished brilliance of enamel. In all his writings, and naturally most of all in his verse, Gautier was intensely preoccupied with style. These poems were incessantly corrected, and incessantly improved. Though they are marked by such austerity of art, there is here and there a personal note in them that is more pronounced and more poignant than in Gautier's prose. His heart was in his poetry. ' If I had possessed any personal fortune,' he wrote to Sainte-Beuve, ' I should have devoted myself wholly to the green laurel.'

A few of his shorter poems will live as long as the language. Gautier was, in fact, one of those poets of the second rank such as he himself delighted to study and appraise—one of those poets who have written a few immortal lyrics which are found in every anthology. When we think of him we are constantly reminded—notwithstanding the wide differences that make the comparison seem fantastic—of our own minor poets of the seventeenth century, of Shirley and Lovelace and Crashaw, poets who had a limited range but a marvellous style, and each of whom wrote a few poems that are of a flawless perfection. In recondite fancy, in verbal felicity, in grace of form, in precision of art, there is a real parallel between the Frenchman and the best of our Caroline and Jacobean poets.

One of his most delightful poems, which might well be selected as representative of Gautier's peculiar charm, is the famous *Chanson d'Automne*. It illustrates several of the characteristics which have already been described—his love of travel, his passion for colour, and his quaint erudition, with a pathetic touch of his personal longing for liberty and leisure. The swallows on the roof are gossiping to one another about the places where they will spend the winter. One will build her nest in a cracked cornice of the Parthenon at Athens, another on the crest of a pillar in the Palace of the Knights at Rhodes ; one flies to Malta, another to Cairo, another to Smyrna :

> Then all : ' What strange scenes we shall view,
>   Each flying to our southern home ;
> Brown plains, white peaks, and seas of blue,
>   And beaches edged with foam ! '
>
> I know all that the swallows say,
>   For poets, too, are birds ; and I,
> A captive bird, lament to-day
>   Because I cannot fly.
>
> Wings ! Wings ! I think of Rückert's song,
>   And wish that I could fly away
> To seek with all the feathered throng
>   Green spring and golden day !

Gautier's poetical testament is given to the world in the magnificent verses entitled *L'Art*. What he believed and what he practised is all here ; the artist's skill and patience and conscience, and an undying faith in beauty. It is true that the artist cannot dispense with inspiration, but it is equally true that there does not exist any substitute for skill. The poet, the painter, the sculptor, only reaches the height of his art by a resolute effort after precision—a victorious struggle with a difficult medium, enamel, marble, onyx, verse.

> Strive with the stubborn stone, until
>   The imprisoned loveliness escape,
> And, through your skill,
>   Become a pure and permanent shape.
>
> Borrow the bronze from Syracuse
>   Wherewith to make your work abide,
> And thence infuse
>   The metal with a classic pride.
>
> All else is destined to the dust,
>   But art is of a deathless date :
> The marble bust
>   Survives the city and the state.
>
> The medal buried in the soil
>   Found by some tiller of the vine,
> Bent at his toil,
>   Reveals an austere Antonine.
>
> The very gods themselves must die,
>   And all things change, as ages pass ;
> Yet poesy
>   Remains, more durable than brass.
>
> But art is long ; carve, chisel, file,
>   Till the reluctant mass shall seem
> Alert, agile,
>   The substance of your floating dream !

VIII

WHAT IS POETRY ?

Rien de ce qui ne transporte pas n'est poésie. La lyre est un instrument ailé.

Joubert.

VIII

WHAT IS POETRY?

WHAT is poetry? The answer is not to be given as easily as might appear at first, even if we leave out of account the more debatable kind of verse and restrict our consideration to the great writings of the great poets. For that wonderful treasury of imaginative literature which is accepted by the intellectual world as poetry is plainly of many kinds and in many modes. There is no single standard that will apply to the whole mass equally, or even to the larger part of it. Whatever your definition of the poetical may be, there are passages which must be described as unpoetical in the greatest poems that have ever been written, and that is only saying that there are parts of these immortal poems that are not really poetry. Then what is essential poetry? What is it that constitutes sheer, absolute, final poetry?

The answer must depend, in a large degree, upon a distinction that is involved in the very nature of poetry, as of all things else—the distinction between form and spirit. It ought to be obvious that whatever our definition of poetry may be, it necessarily involves what must be called form, and that in a double sense. In the higher sense it involves beauty of expression. Language is the medium of poetry, and beauty of language is as necessary in poetry as beauty of shape

141

and beauty of colour are in pictorial art. That will probably be conceded by everyone, whatever his theory of poetry may be, except a few distracted modernists who make a fetich of ugliness in words as in other things. But form is necessary also in the lower sense of the term. For poetry, as an art, involves not only the use of beautiful language, but also the use of measured language : whether it depends upon quantity or accent, assonance or rhyme, it necessarily means the use of set measures of speech. There is, of course, a definite revolt against this principle in our days. The almost shapeless verse of some modern writers, and the definite cult of *vers libre* is not mere inability to use the forms of verse, as one might malignantly suppose ; it is a deliberate protest against what is viewed as the tyranny of poetic form. It is a most irrational protest, all the same. As Mr. Chesterton once said, it is precisely like lying in a dry ditch and talking of free architecture. A man has every right to compose prose fancies which are poetical in intention, but he has no right at all to call them verse, whether free or otherwise. Similarly, a person has a perfect right to indulge in irregular movements of the body which he considers graceful, but unless there is rhythm in the movements, that is to say, some regular rule, some order and measure and recurrence, he is not dancing, and it is merely ridiculous to call those movements by that name. The fact is that there must be an element of artificiality in all art. One is always tempted to sympathize with revolt against convention, and when the conventions have become too narrow and too rigid, the revolt is a very healthy event. But it must not be forgotten that convention cannot be wholly escaped. There is an irreducible minimum of it that is not to be evaded, if the arts are to be continued at all. However you seek to denude the drama of dramatic conventions, it still pictures events in what is, strictly, an artificial and indeed an impossible fashion : people do not sit talking in a drawing-room one wall of which has been taken out, nor soliloquize on the most intimate matters within hearing of a thousand people. Unless that sort of artificiality is frankly accepted—unless it is taken for granted at the beginning and assumed all through—there is an end of all dramatic art. And so with all the other arts ; each has, and must have, its admitted conventions, the specially conceded artificialities that make it an art. There is an element of the artificial, in this sense, in all poetic diction. For poetry is not a simple, direct, unaffected way of speech.[1] If it were, it would be prose, and prose of the kind that M. Jourdain had been talking all his life without knowing what it was. Nothing is more instructive on this particular issue than the relation between Wordsworth's principles and his practice. In his revolt against the stiff conventions of eighteenth-century poetry he decided, as the definite and deliberate principle of his own poetic writings, ' to choose incidents and situations from common life, and to relate or describe them throughout,

[1] The critical faculty of the elder Mr. Weller had discerned this. 'Tain't in poetry, is it ? ' said he. ' No, no,' replied Sam. ' Wery glad to hear it,' said Mr. Weller. ' Poetry's unnat'ral ; no man ever talked poetry 'cept a beadle on boxin' day, or Warren's blackin', or Rowland's oil, or some o' them low fellows. Never you let yourself down to talk poetry, my boy. Begin agin, Sammy.'

as far as was possible, in a selection of language really used by men.' [1] Now sometimes Wordsworth was true to the very letter of his theory, and the result was verses such as *The Idiot Boy*—verses which lent themselves so infallibly to parody like that of the *Rejected Addresses :*

> My father's walls are made of brick,
> But not so tall and not so thick
>   As these ; and, goodness me !
> My father's beams are made of wood,
> But never, never half so good
>   As those that now I see !

But in all his best poetry he was better than his theory. No poor widow lamenting her lost son ever cried :

> 'Tis falsely said
> That there was ever intercourse
> Between the living and the dead ;
> For, surely, then I should have sight
> Of him I wait for day and night
> With love and longings infinite.

The sentiment is deeply true, and what any bereaved mother might feel, but no unlettered woman would express herself like that. There is not only nobility in the language—there is art, as any analysis of the sounds will show. And all poetic diction is artificial in the same way—there is artifice in it, more or less conscious. It is still more plainly true that metre and rhyme are artificial. Poetry is not merely artistic language, in that the words are happily chosen and delicately poised, both in sound and sense, but it is language arranged within artificial patterns. And the simple truth is that there cannot be poetry, in any

[1] Preface to the Second Edition of the *Lyrical Ballads.*

intelligible meaning of the word, without metrical
form. If that form implies tyranny, and the anarchic
soul of the modern writer rebels against it, let him
abolish poetry :

> Après la croix, brise la lyre,
> Peuple, si tu hais les tyrans.

But the regularity, the rhythm, the restraint of
measured language must be present, if there is to be
poetry at all.

The opposite side of the truth scarcely needs urging,
least of all perhaps in our days. The spirit is as
necessary as the form, and obviously much more vital.
The form may be technically perfect, and yet the
verse may be dead. What the life of poetry, the
very soul of poetry is, it is perhaps impossible to say
without either rhapsodizing, or borrowing the language
of the great poets themselves. It is an indescribable
imaginative vitality and vividness, the very life of
the poet's mind passing into his verse. As Silvius
says of love :

> It is to be all made of fantasy,
> All made of passion, and all made of wishes.

It is a sense of beauty so deeply felt that it becomes
possessed by a quality that is at once passionate and
universal. Thus, in its highest moments, it is an
almost religious affirmation of the infinite splendour
of the life of the universe around us, and of the still
nobler glories of the mind.

Now it is not to be denied that the form and the
spirit may exist apart. Are the following lines poetry ?
They are blank verse, and they scan : moreover they

are a part of a great poem, as no one is likely to deny, but are they poetry ?

> Pietro at least had done no harm, I know ;
> Nor even Violante, so much harm as makes
> Such revenge lawful. Certainly she erred—
> Did wrong, how shall I dare say otherwise ?
> In telling that first falsehood, buying me
> From my poor faulty mother at a price
> To pass off upon Pietro as his child.[1]

Surely no competent critic would contend that these lines are essential poetry, or that they are poetry in any sense except the conventional one—that they possess the form of verse.

Again, is the following passage poetry ? ' But we have other sources of power, in the imagery of our iron coasts and azure hills ; of power more pure, nor less serene, than that of the hermit spirit which once lighted with white lines of cloisters the glades of the Alpine pine, and raised into ordered spires the wild rocks of the Norman sea ; which gave to the temple gate the depth and darkness of Elijah's Horeb cave ; and lifted out of the populous city, gray cliffs of lonely stone, into the midst of sailing birds and silent air.'[2] Surely, again, no one who knows what poetry is would deny for a moment that the spirit of poetry is in this passage, the high imaginative quality allied with lofty language which is the very essence of poetry : and yet the paragraph is not poetry, because it has not the proper form, the regular rhythm, of verse.

We must say, then, that it is possible to have prosaic verse, and that it is possible to have poetical prose ;

[1] *The Ring and the Book*, vii. 268–274.
[2] *Seven Lamps of Architecture*, iii. 24.

the form without the spirit and the spirit without the form. But it is only where they are found together, and where they are fused into one, that there is essential poetry.

That is to say, in other words, there must be beauty of conception and beauty of expression, and both within the necessary canons of the poetic art. A thing may be beautifully conceived and beautifully executed in colour and on canvas, but it is not sculpture, because the necessary form of sculpture is in relief : that is what men have always meant by sculpture, and unless we mean that we ought not to use the term. Now you may have the spirit of poetry beautifully expressed, but if it is expressed in words which do not possess some regular and recurrent rhythm, it is not poetry, because that rhythm is the necessary form of poetry ; if it is not present, the product is not what has always been meant by poetry, and if we do not mean that it is mere perversity to use the word.

The definition of absolute poetry, then, would seem to involve at least these elements—beautiful thought, beautiful language, and rhythmic form. Each may conceivably exist alone, and each alone does not constitute poetry. Beautiful thought poorly expressed is not poetry. Beautiful language expressing poor thought is not poetry. Mere rhythm apart from thought and language is not poetry. But where these are fused into one in a kind of spiritual fervour, in that imaginative passion that we call inspiration—there, and there alone, we have essential poetry.

This means that absolute poetry is lyrical, and, indeed, that conclusion would seem to be quite natural and quite inevitable.   But it has often been attacked, and notably by one who is himself a considerable poet, as well as an able and accomplished critic, Mr. Lascelles Abercrombie, in a recent book.   Mr. Abercrombie recurs to the attack so often that it might be said that this is the real thesis of the book.   ' There is a heresy, very prevalent nowadays,' he writes, ' the doctrine that poetry can only be lyrical ; even epics and dramas, this doctrine supposes, can only justify themselves as poetry by their lyrical moments, their suddenly kindled raptures of imagination that detach themselves and escape from a non-lyrical purpose.' [1] Again :   ' Poetry preserves its purity so long as it resides in those prime immediacies of sense, feeling, imagination, which, once poetry has *said* them, leave us nothing to say *about* them.   That is the argument ; and there is nothing wrong with it except that by *poetry* it means *lyrical poetry*.   One may perhaps prefer lyrical poetry to all other kinds ; but the didactic heresy itself was not more arbitrary and illogical than the attempt to confine the scope of poetry within its lyrical effort.' [2]   And again :   ' To regard such a poem as *The Tragical History of Dr. Faustus* as justified merely by detachable lyrical moments, however splendid these may be, is to take the means for the end, to put substance above form ; and that is to ignore a vital part of what the lyrical moments themselves have to say to us :   for you cannot see all they mean until you can see their place and function in the whole poem.' [3]

[1] *The Idea of Great Poetry*, pp. 64–65.
[2] *Ibid.*, pp. 14–15.   [3] *Ibid.*, p. 69.

Now it is plain that there are some factors described in the above paragraphs of which serious account must be taken, and we may congratulate ourselves that everything adverse to the lyrical theory of poetry is said here as directly and as effectively as it is ever likely to be said.

But for our part we should frankly accept the challenge and say that what is absolute poetry in one of Marlowe's or Shakespeare's plays, for example, does consist precisely in their lyrical moments, their ' suddenly kindled raptures of imagination,' which, as Mr. Abercrombie admits, ' detach themselves and escape.' We should say, without a blush, that it is not poetry at all when Perdita says :

>   These are flowers
> Of middle summer, and I think they are given
> To men of middle age. You're very welcome,

and that it is poetry of the most absolute kind when she says, a few lines farther on :

>   O Proserpina,
> For the flowers now, that frighted thou let'st fall
> From Dis's waggon ! daffodils,
> That come before the swallow dares, and take
> The winds of March with beauty ; violets dim,
> But sweeter than the lids of Juno's eyes
> Or Cytherea's breath.

From this point of view, one of Shakespeare's plays, as a whole, is only classed as poetry because it is written in metre, and only becomes actually and absolutely poetry in lyrical passages such as the splendid and familiar lines which have been quoted.

But that, of course, is not the whole of the truth,

for these lyrical passages gain something from their place and purpose in the whole play. The gems have their setting. And this introduces the whole fact of structure as apart from execution. The architectural design of a great cathedral may be one of surpassing beauty, but it is necessarily on so vast a scale that many things which need not be really beautiful in themselves become subservient to the beauty of the whole. The blank stretches of wall, the heavy pillars, the hideous gargoyles, may all become a part of the ordered splendour of the whole shrine. And so in one of Shakespeare's plays the pedestrian passages which are necessary to carry on the dramatic action, the witty sayings of a courtier, the nonsense of a clown or the quips of a fool, all help to fulfil the entire design, which may perhaps be called, for the sake of argument, poetical in conception, while some of these details are not. But surely even if the whole design is poetical that does not make every line in the play pure poetry, any more than the fact that the whole design of the minster is beautiful makes every single stone in it beautiful. And so we are back again at the old issue, for if some parts of the play are absolute poetry and some are not, there will be no doubt at all in anyone's mind that it is the lyrical passages that are really poetry, and the rest of the play that is not.

But, to deal with this matter of structure in more detail, it may well be asked, Is there any thing that can be strictly called poetical in the larger structure of a poem or a play? Apart from the execution, and looking merely at the fabric of the poem, is not the structure of the *Odyssey* simply that of a folk-tale?

And if the adventures of Ulysses had been related in prose, in an old Byzantine legend, would not all the poetry have vanished ? On the other hand, if one of Malory's tales had been put into verse by Spenser, would it not (in proportion to the degree of the poet's inspiration and the success of his execution) have become poetry ? They would both have been heroic stories still, but the one would have become less than a poem, and the other more than a tale.   The epic and the drama, in fact, may be executed in prose as well as in poetry, and therefore it is not the heroic narrative nor the dramatic quality that constitutes these forms of literature poetry, but the poetic spirit which informs them, and the poetic language which clothes them.   And where these are fused you have the epic or the drama passing, for a moment, into a lyric.   It is humanly impossible for the pure poetic spirit and the perfect poetic expression to coalesce into absolute unity for thousands of lines together ; hence the truth of Edgar Allan Poe's paradox that ' a long poem is a contradiction in terms.'   But they may be, and are, blended in moments of high inspiration, and then the verse kindles and becomes lyrical, and what has been called poetry, by a courtesy title, becomes really poetry, absolute poetry, the poetry of inspiration.

It seems impossible to regard the total design of a work as poetical, apart from the execution of it. The whole conception may indeed be one of beauty or of sublimity, but the beautiful or the sublime is not necessarily poetical in itself. If *Paradise Lost* had been executed in prose by John Bunyan, the whole design might have been nobly accomplished, yet that would not have made it poetry. But if John Milton had executed the *Pilgrim's Progress* in blank verse, while the whole scheme of the narrative might again have been preserved unaltered, it is safe to say that the allegory would have become stately poetry. It seems manifest that there is nothing in the total design of an epic or a drama that is necessarily or exclusively of the essence of poetry. The imaginative grandeur of such a scheme is indeed a great achievement in literature, but it does not constitute poetry.

On the other hand, it is both an argument of intellectual greatness in the writer, and a noble setting for the lyrical utterances of a great writer who is also a great poet. This is the real argument against ' those odd compilations, once so popular in drawing-rooms, *Beauties of Shakespeare*, *Beauties of Spenser*, and the like,' which Mr. Abercrombie properly scorns. It is not that such a compilation, if properly selected, might not contain all the pure poetry in Shakespeare, but that the pure gold lacks its setting—a setting which is not of the same texture, but which places the precious metal in its right perspective and throws it into its proper relief. It is true that a splendid line from the *Paradiso* owes much to the splendour of the whole vision which it helps to illustrate, and loses much when it stands by itself, isolated both as a sentiment and as an utterance. But it is also true that if every splendid line were taken out of the *Paradiso* the vision would fade ; if the verse all became mediocre, the whole glory of the conception would be dimmed into the commonplace.

Does not the whole history of our own literature

illustrate the truth of this thesis as to the lyrical spirit constituting the essence of all real poetry ?   All whose judgement is worth anything would probably agree that the two great heights in English poetry, the twin peaks of our Parnassus, are represented by the Elizabethan poets who gather around Shakespeare, and by the modern poets who belong to the half-century or so following the publication of the *Lyrical Ballads*.   And these are precisely the lyrical epochs.   The lyrical impulse which is seen in Chaucer rises to its height in Shakespeare, becomes more deliberate and conscious in the lyrists of the seventeenth century, dies out utterly in the middle of the eighteenth century, is reborn in *The Ancient Mariner* and *Tintern Abbey*, and expends itself once more in the great Victorians. Our poetry, that is to say, is real poetry, essential poetry, in proportion to the presence of the lyrical spirit.   When that spirit has departed, it is not poetry at all.   In what sense is Pope's verse poetry ?   Merely in the sense that it is written in metre and in rhyme. It is verse, in short, and not poetry ; witty, clever, polished, and exceedingly quotable verse, but it is a profanation of the word to call it poetry.   Except that the form of the couplet helps the antithetical and epigrammatic style, and that the rhyme lends it an additional snap, Pope's verse might as well have been written in prose.

This theory of poetry seems to us the only possible one.   The difficulty that it presents to some critics lies in the fact that it is an ' attempt to confine the scope of poetry within its lyrical effort,' as Mr. Abercrombie says.   But does the objection really mean anything more than that the minds of men are still haunted by the traditional classification of poetry into different kinds as epic, dramatic, didactic, lyrical, and so on ? And can that still be seriously maintained as a real and organic classification of poetry ?   The terms are useful terms, of course, but, except the last, they do not indicate any real difference that is characteristic of poetry and not of prose.   There must be some essential characteristic of poetry, in addition to the formal one of metre, and apart from the mere intellectual distinction which it can share with every possible form of literature ; some vital attribute the presence of which *makes* poetry.   And what is there, except the lyrical quality, to serve as an indubitable characteristic and criterion of essential poetry ?   What is there in common, for example, between *The Tempest, Samson Agonistes, Alexander's Feast, Christabel, St. Agnes' Eve, Tithonus*, and *Abt Vogler* (to mention titles almost haphazard) that can serve as a standard and a definition of what poetry really and essentially is ?   There is nothing in common between these poems except these three things—first, that they are all in verse, a characteristic that they share with the most scandalous doggerel that was ever written ; secondly, that they all exhibit high intellectual power, a characteristic which they share with a great deal of prose, and some very bad prose at that ; and third, that they all possess, here and there, that note of kindled fancy indissolubly blended with apt and noble language that we call the lyrical spirit.   It is that surely, and nothing else, in the last resort, that makes them (to whatever extent they are) absolute and immortal poetry.

IX

JOHN DAVIDSON

The inheritors of unfulfilled renown
Rose from their thrones, built beyond mortal thought,
Far in the Unapparent.

Shelley.

IX

JOHN DAVIDSON

JOHN DAVIDSON is perhaps the most tragic figure in English letters during the last half-century. There are others during that period who come to mind when we think of ' mighty poets in their misery dead,' but there is no man of equal gifts whose destiny was so perverse and whose end was so sad. An inequitable fate has pursued him even since his death, now nearly twenty years ago, for he has never had the posthumous recognition that is his due. We prophesy that sooner or later this is bound to come, and that John Davidson will be ranked with Francis Thompson and Sir William Watson as one of the three poets whose work dates about the beginning of the twentieth century who have elements of indubitable and immortal greatness.

John Davidson was born at Barrhead, in Renfrewshire, on April 11, 1857. His father was the Rev. Alexander Davidson, a minister of the Evangelical Union, a community which seceded from the United Secession Church, in protest against Calvinist doctrine, under the leadership of Dr. James Morison, the distinguished commentator. The elder Davidson was for some time Dr. Morison's colleague in Glasgow, and there part of the poet's early childhood was spent. In the *Ballad of a Poet Born* there is a vivid and poignant sketch of Davidson's father and mother, and

157

of the situation in the home when the youth was growing into manhood—the earnest evangelical piety of the parents, and the lad's rebellion against it, a rebellion which is represented as a passionate quest for beauty and romance, but which was confessedly also a sensual revolt :

> Oh, let me be !
> The dreamer cried, and rushing from the house
> He sought the outcast Aphrodite, dull,
> Tawdry, unbeautiful, but still divine
> Even in the dark streets of a noisome port.

The boy left school at thirteen, and went into the chemical laboratory of a sugar-refining firm, and, the year after, into the office of the borough analyst. When he was fifteen he returned to his old school, the Highlanders' Academy, Greenock, as a pupil teacher, and remained for four years. He managed somehow to attend the University of Edinburgh for one session, and then he spent some years in various schools, engaged in what was evidently the uncongenial task of teaching. He also began to write, and did a good deal of literary work for the *Glasgow Herald*, directed then by men like Mr. Russell, Mr. William Wallace, and Mr. William Canton, who were not only very able journalists but had themselves the literary sense and the literary gift. Then in 1890 he did what so many Scotsmen have done, both in fiction and in fact, before and since : he went up to London with a few letters of introduction, and very little money, leaving his wife and family in Scotland for a time, to throw himself upon the world of literature, and seek fame as a poet. For some four or five years he had a stern struggle. On the recommendation of George Meredith, to whom he had sent some of his writings, he got a good deal of reviewing to do for the *Academy*, and later for the *Speaker*. Of the latter journal he was sub-editor for a time, in succession to Mr. Barry Pain. His genius and temperament did not fit him, however, for the life of journalism. Mr. Richard Whiteing once related an incident which illustrates this. When he was on the staff of the *Daily News*, Mr. Whiteing went away for a holiday, and Davidson took his place. The first evening the poet was asked to write a leader paragraph. It was produced with some mental effort, and handed to the editor, who pointed out in the kindest manner that it was too discursive to arrest the average reader's attention. A moment or two later, Davidson said, ' Do you know, I think I won't stay,' and in spite of all entreaties, he insisted on leaving the office then and there. As he reached the door he turned back with the request, ' Oh, by the way, I should like that abortive essay. I may be able to use it one of these days in a novel.' A trivial incident like this (which does not stand alone) is enough to shew how greatly his proud, shy, sensitive spirit was unfitted for the rough-and-ready work of journalism.

His first real recognition came with the publication of *Fleet Street Eclogues* in 1893. This volume and a second volume under the same title which appeared in 1896, contain, in our judgement, some of his very best work. He once gave, in an interview, an account of the inception of this series of poems. ' When I was a teacher in Scotland,' he said, ' I had the idea of writing a kind of teacher's calendar on the plan of the old

Shepherd's Calendar, but this idea was never carried out.   When my father died, however, among the books that came into my possession was a copy of Gibbon's *Decline and Fall*.   As I read it the old idea revived, but I was in London now, and the journalists of Fleet Street seemed closer friends than the teachers of my younger days.   So I wrote a journalist's calendar, under the title of *Fleet Street Eclogues*, and every morning, before sitting down to my desk, I read a chapter of Gibbon.'   It is quite possible, by the way, to discern the influence of the great historian in the poems.

The revival of the eclogue as a poetical form is an interesting circumstance in itself.   It had scarcely been used in English poetry since the eighteenth century, and then it was merely an affectation—a deliberate and servile imitation of the pastoral poetry of Virgil and other classical writers.   Davidson modernized it and made of it a poetical medium that was really effective and really beautiful.   It was a framework into which he could put verse of many moods and of many kinds, didactic, narrative, and lyric, and yet invest the whole with some continuity of interest and with an artistic unity.

The first series of *Fleet Street Eclogues* made Davidson known to the discerning as a poet of power and promise. But he was to make a dramatic entry into a larger fame.   He might have said, like Byron, that he awoke one morning and found himself famous.   It was when his poem, *The Ballad of a Nun*, was published in *The Yellow Book*.   (It may be necessary to explain to those whose memories do not reach back thirty years that this was a literary quarterly published by Mr. John Lane which was supposed, especially in its early days, to be quite startlingly decadent and *fin de siècle*, as the phrase went. It owed that particular reputation very largely to the fact that it was identified, on the artistic side, with the morbid work of Aubrey Beardsley. But *The Yellow Book* is sure of a niche in the history of our literature, if only because it published, in one number, Sir William Watson's noble *Hymn to the Sea*, and Davidson's *St. George's Day*, one of the best of his eclogues. This, however, was a little later than the time of which we are speaking.) When *The Ballad of a Nun* appeared there was a *furore* such as perhaps no single poem has produced for a couple of generations past. John Davidson's name was on everybody's lips. There were portraits of him, interviews with him, articles about him, in all the literary papers. It looked as if his fame and fortune were both made.

Ballads and Songs, which came out in 1894, on the heels of the sensation made by this poem, is probably the most popular of all the volumes of Davidson's poetry. It contained *The Ballad of a Nun*, and some other striking verse, but not, at least in our judgement, either the best or the most typical of the poet's work. Two other volumes of verse appeared within the next few years, *New Ballads*, in 1897, and *The Last Ballad* in 1899.

In these years, however, there was an interlude devoted to the theatre. Davidson had written several plays—his earliest work, while he was yet a teacher in Scotland, was a quartette of plays—and later in life he was to write a couple more, but none of his own plays

II

was ever acted. In 1896, however, Mr. Forbes-Robertson (as he was then), who had been much impressed by François Coppée's *Pour la Couronne*, commissioned Davidson (on the advice of Mr. Pinero) to translate it. The play was produced, entitled *For the Crown*, at the Lyceum Theatre in 1896. It is an extraordinarily good version. Coppée's rhymed alexandrines are rendered into powerful and musical blank verse. There is one astonishing *tour-de-force* in Davidson's version—surely one of the most successful pieces of translation ever accomplished in English—a rhymed version of Sophia's famous *papillon* song. It is amazingly literal, and, at the same time, a genuine poem, perhaps even more beautiful than the original. When the play was produced this was not sung, but very effectively recited by Mrs. Patrick Campbell.

Then in 1901 Davidson undertook a translation of Victor Hugo's *Ruy Blas*, at the request of Mr. Lewis Waller. It was produced at the Imperial Theatre, Westminster, in 1904, under the title, *A Queen's Romance*. It is a good version of the play, though, because of the very character of the drama, there is not so much scope for either execution or effect of a poetic kind as in the case of Coppée's play.

About the beginning of the century Davidson began to produce a series of poems in blank verse of which it is difficult to find any sane and sympathetic interpretation. He called them *Testaments*, and they are intended as a serious and deliberate expression of his philosophy of life. The influence of Wagner and Ibsen had been apparent in his poems for years, but latterly he had been under the spell of Nietzsche. He would have been stirred to frenzy if it had been suggested that he owed his doctrine to Nietzsche, but there is no doubt that to a very large extent he did. Davidson did not read German, but the English translations of *Also sprach Zarathustra* and some other of Nietzsche's writings have coloured deeply, and most unhappily, the whole of his later thought. His early scientific studies and his revolt from Christianity led him in the direction of a rather weird materialism, and upon this was grafted the doctrine of the *Uebermensch*. The result was a philosophic egomania which—to speak plainly—was either insanity, or something on the very verge of it. This mad gospel he proclaimed in rhetorical verse (which occasionally has fine passages) and embodied in *The Testament of a Vivisector* (1901), *The Testament of a Man Forbid* (1901), *The Testament of an Empire Builder* (1902), *The Testament of a Prime Minister* (1903), and *The Testament of John Davidson* (1908). He meant to give final expression to his demented creed in a trilogy of plays entitled *God and Mammon*, but only two of the three were written, *The Triumph of Mammon* (1907), and *Mammon and his Message* (1908).

In 1906 he was given a Civil List pension of £100. He was harassed by poverty, still, for his books had never produced any considerable income. He seems also to have suffered from increasing ill-health, and was haunted by the fear of malignant disease. In 1908 he went to live at Penzance. On March 23 in the following year he disappeared from his home. There was a hue and cry, and once more John Davidson became famous in the newspapers for a few days.

He had drowned himself. The thought of suicide had been with him for many years. He had written long before :

> My source of strength, though never to myself
> Confessed before, had been the lurking thought
> That poison, or a bullet, or the waves
> Could stop the unendurable ecstasy
> Of pain or pleasure.

His body was recovered in Mount's Bay some six months later, and, in accordance with his expressed wish, he was buried at sea on September 21, 1909.

John Davidson's personal appearance has been graphically described by Mr. Chesterton. ' A small, vivid man, with dark burning eyes and a high colour. . . . One of the black Scotch, dark and passionate, who before Burns and after have given many such dark eyes and dark emotions to the world. But in him the unmistakable strain, Gaelic or whatever it is, was accentuated almost to oddity ; he looked like some swarthy elf. His eyes had that " dancing madness " in them which Stevenson saw in the eyes of Alan Breck, but he sometimes distorted the expression by screwing a monstrous monocle into one of them. A man more unmistakable would have been hard to find.' His portraits have an uncanny inconsistency, for in his earlier days he wore a beard and a wig, both of which he discarded later, allowing his baldness to appear and reducing the beard to a moustache and imperial.

John Davidson's poetical achievement was, in our opinion, more considerable than has been generally recognized. In his best work there is an immediacy, an inspiration, a kind of preternatural insight into the beauty of the world and into the passion of human life, for which the only name is genius. When this is united, as it was in this instance, with a remarkable command of language and of the technique of verse, there are present all the elements of a really great poet, and this, if he had escaped some perverse influences, John Davidson might have been.

There are some characteristics of Davidson's work that stand out for all the world to see. One of these would strike anyone who merely turned over the pages of his books—it is that Davidson's whole artistic life, like Wagner's, was dominated by mediæval legends. *The Ballad of a Nun* is a perverted reading of the famous legend in which the Virgin took the place of the nun who had left the convent for the sinful world. *A New Ballad of Tannhäuser* is an equally perverse rendering of the legend of the Hörselberg. *The Ballad of a Workman* is a fresh and striking treatment of the legend of the Wandering Jew. *The Last Ballad* is based upon the story of Lancelot and Guinevere. *The Ordeal* turns upon the mediaeval ordeal by fire. And there are many references in the *Eclogues* to the legends associated with ecclesiastical festivals, as, for example, the allusion to the Three Kings of Cologne in *Christmas Eve*. It is a curious fact that one so fiercely modern in his whole outlook (and, we may add, so passionately in revolt against religion) as Davidson was, should have been so much obsessed by legends which belong to the ages of faith.

Another striking feature in Davidson's verse is

the influence of Biblical phraseology and of Biblical conceptions that might be called definitely Hebraic. As a youth in the manse Davidson acquired a familiarity with the Bible that shews itself in the turn of many a phrase, and in the almost prophetic fervour of many of his more serious utterances. It is rather singular, though, and perhaps it illuminates the general cast of his thought, that it is the apocalyptic element in Scripture that evidently had most influence upon him. Again and again there are visions of the Day of Judgement and of Heaven and Hell in his poems. It is so in *A Ballad of Heaven* and *A Ballad of Hell*, as the very titles would make us aware ; but it is so also in *The Exodus from Houndsditch*, in *A Ballad of an Artist's Wife*, in *A Woman and her Son*. This marked feature of his imaginative work is all the more striking when we remember that he had moved entirely away from the Christian faith, and that apocalyptic imagery therefore retained for him no sacred suggestiveness—when we remember, moreover, that he deliberately demoralized it all, so that it was not even an ethical metaphor with him, as it was, for example, with Carlyle. Heaven, Hell, and Judgement were doubtless mythical to Carlyle, but he could still use the phrases and the images with a suggestion of the urgent and final importance of right and wrong, whereas Davidson went out of his way in these poems to denude the conceptions of all ethical content, while he still went on using them. We would suggest that one reason for this was that his cosmic philosophy looked forward to such an end of all things as he could best depict in Biblical imagery, with a difference :

Then there was neither death nor birth,
Time ceased ; and through the ether fell
The smoky sun, the leprous earth—
A cinder and an icicle.

No wrathful vials were unsealed ;
Silent, the first things passed away :
No terror reigned ; no trumpet pealed
The dawn of Everlasting Day.

In his early life Davidson soaked himself in Shake-speare, and he went on to acquire a considerable know-ledge of the other Elizabethan dramatists. He owed a good deal in many ways to this discipline. There is something almost Shakespearean in the force and richness of his poetic vocabulary ; no recent English poet has equalled him either in the range of language at his command, or in the masterful way that he uses it. It is difficult to prove statements as to the extent of a writer's vocabulary, but we imagine that everyone who possesses a feeling for words, and is familiar with Davidson's verse, will be impressed by the wealth of his language. There is no doubt either as to the com-pelling (and sometimes violent) fashion in which he can use it. This is accompanied in Davidson by a riotous imagination, and the result is that there are often extravagances both of fancy and of language that degenerate into mere conceits, and recall the seventeenth-century poets. It is a mild example of this when, in *The Ballad of a Nun*, the votaress ex-claims : ' I am sister to the mountains now, And sister to the sun and moon ! ' which was wickedly paraphrased as : ' I am mother-in-law to the North Pole, And aunt to the Equator ! ' There are much

worse instances than this.   What is to be said of such
a stanza as the following ?—

> The hostess of the sky, the moon,
>   Already stoops to entertain
> The golden light of afternoon
>   And the wan earthshine of the plain.

Or a frantic and vulgar metaphor like this ?—

> On river lawns with emerald velvet spread
> The ewes sedately browse the three-piled nap.

Such things are perverse conceits, mere contortions of
the imagination, that remind one of the metaphysical
poets at their worst.   But when all this has been
discounted, there remains a great vigour of imagination
accompanied by a really astonishing wealth and force
of language.   No poet of the last century has surpassed
Davidson, perhaps none has equalled him, in what
George Macdonald once called, in discussing Byron,
' the physical force of words.'

There are some rather interesting topographical
characteristics about Davidson's verse.   He was a
Scotsman, with a Scotsman's proper national pride.
He could boast that he belonged to a land where :

> The very ploughman holds his plough
>   As proudly as a lance,
> The milkmaid bears a dreamy brow
>   Inheriting romance.

But there are not many descriptions of Scottish
landscape in his poetry.   He once said, in conversation,
that he had been deeply impressed by the scenery of
the Ochills, where he used to spend his summer holidays

when a boy (where, among the glens and the mountains, as he wrote :

> I wandered, a belated faun,
> All sense, all wonder, all delight),

and also by the scenery of the Firth of Clyde, beside which so much of his early life was lived. ' When I am alone and not preoccupied, the sweep of the coast between Helensburgh and the entrance to Loch Long comes before me, and however far I may travel in the future no other coast can be so deeply graven on my memory.' A poem which is manifestly autobiographical begins :

> His father's house looked out across a firth
> Broad-bosomed like a mere, beside a town
> Far in the North.

And in *Lammas* there is a glimpse of Edinburgh through the fog that drapes :

> —— with ghostly tapestry the stones
> Of bleak Tantallon,

and the smoke that hangs over :

> —— The humming Canongate, and flings
> Dusky festoons that wither as they fall
> About the wasted towers of Holyrood.

But there are not many touches of this kind. On the other hand, he knew very well some parts of southern and western England, especially the district around the Cinque Ports and the Quantocks, and London

laid its spell upon him.   One of his poems is entitled
A Cinque Port, and ends upon a note of desolation :

> Below the down the stranded town
>   Hears far away the rollers beat,
> About the wall the sea-birds call ;
>   The salt wind murmurs through the street ;
> Forlorn the sea's forsaken bride
> Awaits the end that shall betide.

Another poem, *In Romney Marsh*, describes a walk
in the same region :

> Shrill blew the wind ; and shrill the wire
>   Rang out from Hythe to Romney town.

In *Midsummer Day*, when 'the west wind blows
about the park, And faintly stirs the Fleet Street
wires,' one of the journalists says :

> —— of many a western mead
> And hill and stream it speaks to me.

> With rosy showers of apple-bloom
>   The orchard sward is mantled deep ;
> Shaded in some sequestered coombe
>   The red deer in the Quantocks sleep.

That remarkable poem, *A Runnable Stag*, is also
framed throughout on a landscape of the West—' the
Priory coombe,' and ' the Charlock glen,' and ' the
Severn Sea.'

But London obsessed Davidson.   He wrote im-
partially of Hampton Court and the Isle of Dogs, of
the Crystal Palace and Houndsditch, of Primrose Hill
and Liverpool Street Station, of Epping Forest and
Regent's Park, of :

> —— the ceaseless roar
> Of wheels and wearied hoofs and wearied feet
> That sounded hoarse behind 'twixt shore and shore
> Of brimming Aldgate Street,

and of the new suburb where :

> —— the whetted fangs of change
> Daily devour the old demesne—
> The busy farm, the quiet grange,
> The wayside inn, the village green.

From a northern height he sees where in the distance :

> Dissolving, dimly reappearing,
> Afloat upon ethereal tides
> St. Paul's above the city rides !

and hears in :

> The million-peopled lanes and alleys
> An ever-muttering prisoned storm,
> The heart of London beating warm.

But it was of Fleet Street that he wrote most of all, ' that most famous faubourg of the world,' as he called it :

> ——the street that counts
> Seven hundred paces of tesselated road
> From Ludgate Circus west to Chancery Lane,

that ' little, noisy London street ' which ' serves as the Dionysius' ear of the world.' It would be comic, if it were not so oddly pathetic, that even here his perverse philosophy forces itself in, and in more than one poem he has to remind us that :

> ——in the nebula of our solar scheme
> Fleet Street and Saturn's rings were interfused,

and that the telegraph-wires and the printing machines and the brick and mortar and the journalists' brains and the street drains of Fleet Street were all :

> —— but exquisite flame
> In the nebula once ere day and night
> Began their travail, or earth became,
> And all was passionate light,

which may be true enough, but hardly deserves the poetic and philosophic prominence that Davidson gives it.   He was obsessed by the nebula; it would be a curious task to count up the number of times that the word occurs in his poems.   This apart, however, he seems to have had a genuine delight in Fleet Street, and in the romantic side of journalism, if not in the actual work itself.   Journalists are the modern adventurers, the knights-errant of to-day:

> —— strong and splendid
> Is the subtle might we wield;
> Though chivalry be ended
> There are champions in the field,

and we may yet see:

> When time shall have unfurled
> His heavy, hanging mists,
> How the future of the world
> Was shaped by journalists.

No doubt it is generally true that Davidson's poetry is marked by exuberance rather than by precision. It belongs definitely to the romantic rather than to the classical tradition : it is rich and forceful rather than disciplined and graceful.   In this Davidson was a complete and striking counterpart to his distinguished contemporary, Sir William Watson.   Yet it is worthy of remark that upon occasion, when he took the trouble, Davidson could write verse of a rather difficult structure which was yet technically perfect.   He had been largely under the influence of Poe in his later years, though he was so impatient of being thought any man's disciple that he has deliberately made disparaging remarks somewhere about the American poet.

But there can be no doubt at all as to Poe's influence upon Davidson's technique. A poem like *A Runnable Stag*, with its artfully varied refrains and its internal rhymes, is reminiscent of Poe throughout. So is *The Lutanist*, so is *Bartlemas*, and so, to a less extent, is *Serenade*. And there are other examples of the same technical influence.

Davidson's mind, as we have hinted already, was richer in its creative than in its critical faculty. His verse would have been vastly the better for a strict revision by someone whose poetic taste was severe. He could write magnificently, and he could write abominably, and apparently he did not know when he was at his best or at his worst. He could compass the astonishing music of such a stanza as:

> The trumpets pealed ; the echoes sang
> A tossing fugue ; before it died
> Again the rending trumpets rang,
> Again the phantom notes replied.

But he could also write a tortured screed like this:

> A morbid, acidulent scorn
> Inhabits the vinegared lees
> In bosoms condignly forlorn—
> In bosoms philosophy frees
> From the burden to which we are born !

He was quite capable, also, of defending his worst verses as irreproachable, and of describing all criticism of them (as he once did in a letter to me one of Dr. Garnett's critical remarks upon a stanza in *The Ballad of a Nun*) as ' a piece of dull pedantry.' If he would have criticized himself with some detachment and deliberation, he would have been a much greater

writer. Because he lacked either the power or the
will to do it, he wrote a good deal that was mediocre ;
much of his later blank verse particularly is merely
turgid rhetoric. Sometimes, too, a really fine stanza
is half ruined by some unhappy phrase, as in the
delightful vignette of winter :

> In holly hedges starving birds
>   Silently mourn the setting year.
> Upright like silver-plated swords
>   The flags stand in the frozen mere.

The last lines may serve also to remind us that
Davidson had a real passion for Nature, though it was
very different from that which we associate with
Wordsworth. He had a sensuous delight in the sights
and sounds of the world. He could say of himself,
and the words are illustrated on almost every page
that he wrote :

> I am besieged by things that I have seen :
> Followed and watched by rivers ; snared and held
> In labyrinthine woods and tangled meads ;
> Hemmed in by mountains ; waylaid by the sun ;
> Environed and beset by moon and stars ;
> Whispered by winds and summoned by the sea.

Few of our poets have been so exact in their
observation or so discerning in their description of
natural life. It would take a professed naturalist to
comment suitably upon the minute sketches of birds
and flowers that appear in the poems. But anyone
can see how vivid and picturesque, how intensely *seen*
by the poet's eye, is a description like this :

> Where ribbed and spiny hedges
>   Hold fast the empty ear,
> Or where like summer's pledges
>   The ruddy hips appear.

Or this :

> The dripping ivy drapes the walls ;
>   The drenched red creepers flare ;
> And the draggled chestnut plumage falls
>   In every park and square.

Or this :

> Motionless leaden cloud
>   The region roofed and walled ;
> Beneath, a tempest shrieked aloud
>   And the forest beckoned and called.

But there can be no question about the reality of Davidson's poetic genius. If anyone doubts it let him read the splendid rhapsody about fairy-land, in *All Hallows' Eve*, beginning :

> No, oh no !
> In Elfland is no rest,
> But rumour and stir and endless woe
>   Of the unfulfilled behest—
> The doleful yoke of the Elfin folk
>   Since first the sun went west,

or the superb lament over the evils of civilization in *St. George's Day*, which begins :

> I see the strong coerce the weak,
>   And labour overwrought rebel,
> I hear the useless treadmill creak,
>   The prisoner, cursing in his cell,

and ends :

> Hoarsely they beg of Fate to give
>   A little lightening of their woe,
> A little time to love, to live,
>   A little time to think and know.

We are convinced, for our own part, that at least a handful of Davidson's lyrics are sure of immortality, whatever the vagaries of poetic taste may be for the moment.   Despite his perversities, John Davidson was a man of real genius, and immeasurably greater as a poet than any of the crowd of bizarre nonentities whose productions fill our anthologies of modern verse.

X

DORA GREENWELL

Those rare works where thou shalt leave writ
Love's noble history, with wit
Taught thee by none but Him, while here
They feed our souls, shall clothe thine there.

Crashaw.

X

DORA GREENWELL

It is a significant thing that religious literature, even when it bears the most indubitable marks of genius, often has to wait for general recognition until it has won an express sanction from some literary authority. The *Dies irae, dies illa* of Thomas of Celano never received literary recognition until Goethe used it in *Faust.* Bunyan's *Pilgrim's Progress* was not accounted an English classic until Macaulay pronounced his verdict upon it. The remarkable English of Wesley and the early Methodist preachers, which strikes an absolutely new note both in prose and verse, was never noticed until Edward FitzGerald wrote about it with enthusiasm. So to-day one may look in vain into books dealing with the English literature of the nineteenth century for an appreciation of Dora Greenwell. The authoritative critic who is to be her literary sponsor has not yet arrived. But there cannot be the smallest doubt that she is not only an authority upon the life of the soul, but a really great writer of English prose, and some day, we are sure, the fact will be acclaimed.

Her life was singularly uneventful. She was born on December 6, 1821, at Greenwell Ford, near Lanchester, in the county of Durham. Her father was a country squire in affluent circumstances, and Greenwell

12*   179

X

DORA GREENWELL

It is a significant thing that religious literature, even when it bears the most indubitable marks of genius, often has to wait for general recognition until it has won an express sanction from some literary authority. The *Dies irae, dies illa* of Thomas of Celano never received literary recognition until Goethe used it in *Faust.* Bunyan's *Pilgrim's Progress* was not accounted an English classic until Macaulay pronounced his verdict upon it. The remarkable English of Wesley and the early Methodist preachers, which strikes an absolutely new note both in prose and verse, was never noticed until Edward FitzGerald wrote about it with enthusiasm. So to-day one may look in vain into books dealing with the English literature of the nineteenth century for an appreciation of Dora Greenwell. The authoritative critic who is to be her literary sponsor has not yet arrived. But there cannot be the smallest doubt that she is not only an authority upon the life of the soul, but a really great writer of English prose, and some day, we are sure, the fact will be acclaimed.

Her life was singularly uneventful. She was born on December 6, 1821, at Greenwell Ford, near Lanchester, in the county of Durham. Her father was a country squire in affluent circumstances, and Greenwell

Ford was a country mansion, of the more modest kind, where the family had dwelt for three centuries past. Her mother was the daughter of a lawyer in the city of Durham. Nothing particular seems to be recorded of Dora's education as a girl. Probably all her really effective culture was gained later, and by her own efforts. Dora's father got into financial embarrassments, after her earliest youth was past, and the ancestral home had to be sold. Then she lived for some time at Ovingham Rectory, in the valley of the Tyne, where her elder brother William was holding the living for a friend. Later, from 1850 to 1854, she lived at Golbourne, in Lancashire, where her younger brother Alan had been appointed the first Rector of a new parish. Afterwards, she spent eighteen years in the city of Durham, until the death of her mother, in 1871. Then Dora lived successively in London, Torquay, and Clifton, and finally returned to London in 1882, where she died, on March 29 in that year.

If we judge the matter by ordinary standards a more unfavourable atmosphere can scarcely be imagined, for one of Dora Greenwell's temperament, than the home in which she grew up and spent most of her life. Yet, so strange and subtle are the conditions of the soul's life, that possibly the adverse environment drove her in upon herself and her own religious resources, and so made for solitude and strength of spirit and 'the passion and the life whose fountains are within.' It is manifestly an autobiographical note when a character in one of her books says that her life, for some years, 'partly from want of health, and partly from outward circumstances of a peculiarly

repressive character, had been singularly self-centred,'
and adds that, in such a period, ' while many flowers
had withered, others had come into strange and sudden
bloom.' [1]

Her father seems to have been an amiable person
who did not count for much in his daughter's life,
Her mother was stern, self-righteous, and tyrannical,
without the slightest sympathy for all that was dearest
to Dora—altogether a very unamiable personality.
Of two of her brothers we hear little ; both were
much older than their only sister. Another brother,
William, was a distinguished antiquary and a Canon
of Durham, and died at a very advanced age, not
many years ago. The sympathy between them may
be judged by these two incidents. It is recorded that
she once said to him : ' William, I believe you have
never read one line of my *Carmina Crucis*.' ' And
have you read my *British Barrows* ? ' said he. ' Of
course not,' she replied gravely. ' Of course not,'
said he. And when he gave to her latest biographer
his reminiscences of his sister, long after her death, all
he had to say was depreciatory, and he complained
particularly that ' she was not even a good Church-
woman.' Her younger brother Alan was evidently
the best beloved. He began life as a clergyman,
apparently more or less evangelical, developed into a
High Churchman, got into difficulties with his Bishop,
resigned the ministry, and finally became a Positivist,
to his sister's great distress. Not one member of her
family seems to have had the slightest sense of the
fact that Dora was a spiritual splendour : not one of

[1] *Colloquia Crucis*, p. 9.

them seems even to have suspected that she was a genius.

At least two friendships counted for much in her life. (Perhaps it should be said, to assuage curiosity, that the friend who goes by the name of Philip, in two of her books, is unsubstantial ; he is merely an inter-locutor, and a partial projection of her own personality.) One of those formative friendships was with Josephine Grey of Dilston, afterward famous as Mrs. Josephine Butler. It began in the days spent at Ovingham. Dora Greenwell's first prose volume, *The Patience of Hope*, which dates from ten years after that period, is dedicated to ' J. E. B.' So, one remembers, is F. W. H. Myers' *Saint Paul*. It is a singular tribute to the religious influence of Josephine Butler that two such writers should have acknowledged in such a way how much they owed to her.

The other formative friendship is that which she was happy enough to form with Thomas Constable of Edinburgh, the son of that Archibald Constable who was the friend of Sir Walter Scott. He published her first important book, and an eager friendship grew up between the lonely writer at Durham and the shrewd and kindly publisher and his family at Edinburgh, which brought great joy to them all. Fortunately Thomas Constable was one of the few friends of her daughter who was acceptable to Dora's imperious and repellent mother, so that in this case mutual visits were possible. It is positively pathetic to see how much it meant to Dora to be received as a friend into a kindly, cultured, and religious home where she found both sympathy and admiration.

Considering the circumstances of her life, and her poor health, Dora Greenwell's literary output was rather considerable. Her first volume of verse appeared in 1848, the year the family left the ancestral home. More verses appeared in 1850 and in 1861, and more important volumes of verse followed in the next fifteen years—*Carmina Crucis* in 1869, *Songs of Salvation* in 1873, *The Soul's Legend* in 1873, and *Camera Obscura* in 1876.

Though she wrote so much verse, it cannot be claimed that Dora Greenwell had any real poetical gift. She achieved a few creditable translations, such as the version of Goethe's *Kennst du das Land?*, and some of her original poems have a note of graceful fancy, but it is doubtful whether she ever wrote anything in verse that deserves to live by its own merit, unless it be the lines—the best known of all her verses, probably—which begin :

> I am not skilled to understand
> What God hath willed, what God hath planned ;
> I only know at His right hand
>   Stands One who is my Saviour.

Her earliest prose work was *A Present Heaven*, which appeared in 1855, and was reissued in 1867 as *The Covenant of Life and Peace*. The next was *The Patience of Hope*, published in 1860. This was followed in 1863 by *Two Friends*, and a sequel appeared under the title *Colloquia Crucis*, in 1871. She also published a volume of *Essays* in 1866, and a *Life of Lacordaire* in the following year. She wrote a *Life of John Woolman* in 1871, and another volume of essays with the title *Liber Humanitatis* appeared in 1875. Her last book,

A Basket of Summer Fruit (which is rather a compilation of extracts than an original work) was published
in 1876.

Dora Greenwell was a woman of very considerable
culture.   She was widely read in all sorts of literature
—a careful student of her writings is sometimes startled
to see how wide was her range.   She had studied, for
example, the writings of the more important Fathers
of the Church, as far as they were accessible in translations.   She was an excellent French scholar and
familiar with the best literature in that language.
She read German, and knew at least the greater German
poets.   She read Italian, and enjoyed Dante.   We are
told that she began the study of Latin ; probably she
did not get very far with it, but she confesses that
phrases in the language had a kind of fascination for
her.   Nearly half her books bear Latin titles.   Now
this wide interest in language and literature and the
world of intellect and art generally has a genuine
bearing upon her peculiar achievement as an author.

For the greatness of Dora Greenwell as a devotional
writer might perhaps be defined in a single phrase—she
was an evangelical humanist, and therefore something
of a paradox.   A respectable, moderate, compromising
type of religion can easily accommodate itself to what
Burke called ' the solemn plausibilities of the world,'
and finds no difficulty in adjusting itself not only to
wealth and pleasure, and war and politics, but also to
art and literature.   But whenever religion has been
in deadly earnest, as amongst the first Christians, the
early monks and the early friars, the English Puritans
of the seventeenth century, and the English Evangelicals

of the later eighteenth and the earlier nineteenth
centuries, it has refused compromise, and has stood
for a stark repudiation of the world and all its ways.
Not merely the sinful ways of the world were repre-
hended, but even literature and the arts, as being
less than absolutely spiritual, and as belonging to a
world the fashion of which is passing away. There
are notable exceptions, of whom John Wesley was one,
but the statement is generally true. The result has
been twofold. The evangelical disliked all secular
literature as a kind of vanity, and the man of letters
despised the evangelical faith as a species of fanaticism
Relations were practically broken off, for more than a
century, between the literary world and evangelical
religion.

Now Dora Greenwell was an intense evangelical.
The spiritual truths that are characteristic of evangelical
thought and evangelical experience are the sum and
substance of her teaching. It all gathers around
Christ and Him crucified, and a vital experience of
penitence and faith and forgiveness which is centred
there. Her emblem, which appears on the title-page
of all her books, is a hand grasping a cross, with the
motto, *Et teneo et teneor*, ' I hold and I am held.' To
adapt the titles of two of her books, one might say that
everything she wrote is either a song of the Cross or a
colloquy on the Cross. She might have said herself
what she reports St. Bonaventura as saying, when he
pointed to the crucifix and exclaimed, *Summa Theologia !*

This solemn note in her writings came, as one
would expect, from a deepening of her own religious
thought and experience. Mrs. Josephine Butler wrote,

in a letter of reminiscences addressed to Dora Green-well's latest biographer (in June 1905) : ' At one time I fancied (this was quite early in our friendship) that she did not see clearly the Cross, the merit, the fulness and perfection of the finished work of Christ.   At first she a little differed from me, but later she fully and heartily embraced that great thought, " It is finished," and brought it into her beautiful writings.' [1]   There is a striking passage in one of her books which evidently connects with this—a passage in which she writes of the way that the Cross had become more central in her thought and her experience.   It had entered ' the foreground of her whole existence,' and had become ' the unchanging centre of her thoughts '—so she writes. ' The Cross, as I looked at it more and more intently, became to me the revelation of a loving and a suffering God.   I learnt to look upon the sacrifice of the death of Christ, not only as being the all-sufficient satisfaction for the sins of the whole world, *but also as the everlasting witness to God's sympathy with man.*   The mystery of the Cross did not, it is true, explain any one of the enigmas connected with our mortal existence and destiny, but it linked itself in my spirit with them all. It was itself an enigma flung down by God alongside of the sorrowful problem of human life, the confession of Omnipotence itself to some stern reality of misery and wrong.   *One deep calleth to another.*' [2]   And in a letter to Professor Knight of St. Andrews, dated June 6, 1868, she writes : ' The death of the Saviour remains for me just what it is, a fact ; the one great fact ; in

---

[1] C. L. Maynard, *Dora Greenwell*, pp. 210–11.
[2] *Colloquia Crucis*, p. 13.

itself doubtless an enigma—Heaven's unexplained enigma—but the one which alone to my heart meets and touches all life's direst needs. It is more real than anything in the world, or out of it ; that which brings the pitying, sympathizing element into the whirl and awful chaos of creation ; it makes of God a Being to be loved, because it proves that there is a necessity (of nature unknown to us) for the loss, anguish, and death that presses on the whole world *and that God Himself has stooped to it*. How different from the old gods of Greece, careless and cruel in their continual serenity—*a God upon a Cross*. . . . The aspect in which I see the Cross (since I saw it at all) never varies. It has saved the world, and it will save me.' [1]

But, on the other hand, there is to be found in all Dora Greenwell's work, alongside this deep evangelical faith and this searching evangelical experience, an unfailing love of beauty, of nature and art, of language and literature and romance. One of the most interesting characteristics of her writings, in fact, is her constant preoccupation with the relations between religion and culture. She had a deep and sustained interest in what she herself called ' the connexion of Christianity with poetry, music, nature, with all the purer and more exalted movements of the natural heart.' [2] She was a humanist, in the best sense of the word. Now there is a real and constant danger, for anyone who is so constituted, of minimizing spiritual values in the interest of commending religion to those

[1] C. L. Maynard, *Dora Greenwell*, pp. 212–13.
[2] *Two Friends*, p. 30.

whom Schleiermacher described as its cultured despisers. That is to say, if you are deeply interested in literature and art, and also in religion, you run the risk of reducing the paradoxes of religion, and the stark and poignant facts of sin and redemption—that aspect of experience which was in Wesley's mind when he spoke, in a memorable phrase, of ' the coarse old gospel '—to something more conventional and more complaisant and more amenable to aesthetic treatment. That Dora Greenwell never did. But she felt the natural antagonism, not to be escaped, between the world's art and the world's literature (which, after all, are of the world) and the absolute claims and the unworldly character of vital religion. ' I feel, sometimes painfully,' she writes, ' a contradiction between the brokenness of Christ and the clear perfection of art.' [1] Eager as she rightly was to claim all the kingdoms of the world for Christ, she did not minimize that fundamental disparity. So when Philip had been reading Keats on a delightful summer's afternoon, in the garden, among the scent of flowers, and his conscience sent him to his duty of visiting ignorant folk in stuffy cottages—' Had the world of light and beauty I lived and moved in, but half an hour ago, collapsed into this ! How confused, too, seemed my own statements, my very utterance thick and hesitating as of one under a heavy thrall, *for my heart was with Endymion, and I had to tell the story of Christ.*' [2]

Now a note like that is not often struck in devotional books. It is not to be denied that there is an exotic character about most devotional literature. Many

---

[1] *Two Friends*, p. 43.   [2] *Ibid.*, p. 46.

of the great devotional books suggest the hectic spirituality of the cloister, which ' averts its ken From half of human life,' and only occasionally casts a shuddering glance upon the great world that it despises and deserts. One would scarcely learn from the pages of some spiritual classics that there is a world of beauty and of intellect, a wonderful realm of literature and art, and another world of practical affairs, a sordid region in which most of the life of most men is necessarily passed, both of which must be brought into some intelligible relation to religion, and into a real dependence upon Christ. Now Dora Greenwell, with all her intense preoccupation with the life of the soul, and with all her absolute loyalty to the stern demands of religion, never errs in that deadly fashion. Her outlook is always human ; religion, in her view, is for the whole of man's experience, and nothing that is human is really alien to it. It is true that real religion finds itself at enmity with much in the world, and our author never belittles that fact. No one, indeed, ever recognized it or expressed it more uncompromisingly. ' The rule of Christ,' she writes, ' opposes itself as much to the higher as to the lower instincts of human nature,' and goes on to say that ' the heart can be devoted but to *one* object ; and the winning of the great prizes of earthly endeavour asks for an intensity of purpose, which in the Christian has found another centre.' [1] But even in taking this position, essential to the reality of religion as we believe it to be, Dora Greenwell never ignores and never despises those regions of life and experience

[1] *The Patience of Hope*, p. 24.

that must, in some sense, ' be counted still a heathen land ' ; she never fails to suggest a reason why they are still unredeemed, and she never forgets to look forward to the day when they will be.

What is the secret of Dora Greenwell's remarkable power as a devotional writer ? It has probably been suggested already. It is that rare combination of intellectual and spiritual qualities, which are so often divorced, alas ! There are religious writings that are full of zeal and full of truth, but that have no more title to be called literature (to use R. L. Stevenson's phrase) than Spurgeon's sermons. On the other hand, there are religious writings that have some literary quality, but that are largely destitute of the savour and life of the gospel. Now Dora Greenwell had a cultivated mind, and wrote an admirable style, but she had also a living experience of religion, and an astonishing insight into the human heart, and into all the dealings of God with the human heart. She had a sure and subtle touch in those delicate regions where it is so easy to go wrong, where a fault of accent becomes a failure of reverence, where a supreme truth may be minimized into a mere truism, or ex- aggerated into an immoral lie, where, if you do not go far enough, you have failed to lift the veil, and if you go a step too far, you have profaned the very altar. In such things her instinct was infallible. It is not often that there is found united, in a writer on the spiritual life, so penetrating an insight and so delicate a judgement. There is this quality of subtle and surprising discernment in many of her utterances —an almost uncanny insight into the spiritual life

and its relations to the whole of experience. Here
are some (as we think) striking examples. ' Mere
spirituality seems to exhaust the soil that rears it,
so that Christianity must always gain much from
extraneous sources. It does so, in our own day,
from science and general social progress. These are
its friends, though sometimes disguised ones : and
Christ still gathers where He did not straw, and
reaps where He did not sow.'[1] ' All that we know of
man, whether by tradition or through experience,
shows him to be a being who dreads an unseen foe,
who seeks an unseen friend, one who aspires far above
the present conditions of his nature, and who is yet
capable of being dragged down far beneath them.'[2]
' He would sometimes draw my attention to the strange
alacrity with which the mind, under repressed and
sorrowful circumstances, will draw to itself some small
alleviation, will even create such out of the most adverse
situations. Humanity, he would say, will never consent
to be disinherited of joy ; be it ever so cruelly robbed
and defrauded, it will still put in its persistent claim
to the happiness originally intended for it by God.'[3]
' In the depths of our mortal nature lies a dark un-
sunned well, too deep sunk for the events of common
life to stir and touch it, the waters of which, when
troubled, reflect the Cross, and prepare man's heart
for the cardinal doctrine of Christianity—deliverance
through a work not his own.'[4] ' All things in nature,
as well as all things in grace, point to a Redeemer.
Nature struggles but cannot speak : she remains in

[1] *Two Friends*, p. 128.   [2] *Colloquia Crucis*, p. 135.
[3] *Ibid.*, p. 31.   [4] *Ibid.*, p. 80.

bondage with her children, dumb like them and beautiful. Humanity has found a voice, but where, save for Christ, would it find an answer ? ' [1] If these, and many other passages like them in Dora Greenwell's writings are not utterances of remarkable spiritual insight, expressed in remarkably beautiful English, we are very much deceived.

Where did Dora Greenwell find her wonderful style ? There does not appear to be any evidence, in any of the biographical records, as to any special devotion on her part to particular English writers, such as would suggest any of them as her special favourites and exemplars. We should hazard the conjecture, entirely on internal grounds, that her style owed a good deal to De Quincey, and perhaps something to Hazlitt. These writers are named only once or twice, perhaps, in her books, but we think that anyone who has a feeling for style will probably be reminded of De Quincey as they read, for instance, the visionary passages in the earlier pages of *Two Friends*, and will often think of Hazlitt as they catch the turn of a phrase, and note the adroit use of a quotation. It is impossible to prove a suggestion of this kind, but we have a strong impression that there is some truth in it. Wherever Dora Greenwell got her style, it is an admirable one—strong and flexible and natural, with a frequent felicity in the use of a word or the shape of a phrase, and rising sometimes into a restrained and solemn eloquence.

When an edition of *The Patience of Hope* was issued in the United States in 1862, the poet Whittier wrote

[1] *The Patience of Hope*, p. 30.

an introduction to the book in which he was discerning
enough to class it with the devotional writings of
St. Augustine, à Kempis, Tauler, and Fénelon. If that
estimate be extended to the rest of her more important books—*The Covenant of Life and Peace,
Two Friends*, and *Colloquia Crucis*—we do not believe
it exaggerated. In any case, we are certain that there
has been no devotional writer in English to be compared with Dora Greenwell since the eighteenth and
seventeenth centuries. She stands worthily in the
great fellowship of Charles Wesley, and Samuel
Rutherford, and John Bunyan.